RETSCH's SERIES

OF

TWENTY-SIX OUTLINES,

ILLUSTRATIVE OF

GOETHE's TRAGEDY

OF

FAUST,

ENGRAVED FROM THE ORIGINALS BY HENRY MOSES.

AND AN

ANALYSIS OF THE TRAGEDY

London:

PRINTED FOR BOOSEY AND SONS, BROAD-STREET, EXCHANGE, AND RODWELL AND MARTIN,
NEW BOND STREET.

1820.

W. WILSON, PRINTER, GREVILLE-STREET, HATTON-GARDEN, LONDON.

AN

ANALYSIS

OF

GOETHE's

TRAGEDY OF FAUST,

IN

ILLUSTRATION OF RETSCH's

SERIES OF OUTLINES,

ENGRAVED FROM THE ORIGINALS BY HENRY MOSES.

London:

PRINTED FOR BOOSEY AND SONS, BROAD-STREET, EXCHANGE, AND RODWELL AND MARTIN,
NEW BOND STREET.

1820.

W. WILSON, PRINTER, GREVILLE-STREET, HATTON-GARDEN, LONDON.

AN ANALYSIS

OF

GOETHE's TRAGEDY

OF

FAUST.

INTRODUCTION.

THE Faust of Goethe is perhaps the most original work of German poesy, and one for which his contemporaries are greatly indebted to him. Would you warn the young man who enters upon society, freed from the controul of the school or the superintendance of the tutor—would you point out to him all the dangers to which he will be exposed in the world---you need only give him *Goethe's Faust*, and desire him to read and reflect. The aged, grown grey in years, instead of detailing the results of their experience, will point to the book and say, it comprises all these things. It displays the whole store, discovers the whole abyss of the human heart: it unfolds its most secret recesses---its enjoyments---its cloyed surfeits---and its frivolous wiles, with their direful consequences. As a moral instructor, it ranks with the Cyropaedia of Xenophon, and the Telemachus of Fenelon.

Faust does not represent man as at the time of the Persian prince; not man, as the poet's fancy formed him, for the instruction of a King of the Bourbon race, nor yet the crafty courtier, or worldling, taught by Lord Chesterfield's Letters, deliberately to weigh all his actions between pleasure in one scale, and punishment in the other. *Faust* represents man as he is, in every age, clime, and country;

B

the creature which is a riddle to itself, an enigma, the solution of which has baffled alike the ingenuity of ancient and modern philosophers. This creature " MAN," youth may learn justly to appreciate from *Goethe's* work, and to separate with just discrimination those parts of his exuberant substance, by the nice line which divides good and evil; and thus form within his breast a Temple of the Deity.

Let youth detect the Demon within himself, in order to yield to GOD the sway over his heart, for it appears to us, that the easiest clue to the moral part of this didactic fiction is, to consider Faust and Mephistopheles as *one* person, represented symbolically, only in a two-fold shape.

With respect to the Plates, the artist appears to have acted the part of an ingenious translator, so as it were to renew the work itself, by most intimately adapting his Plates to the very genius of the author. Truth is conspicuous throughout, under all possible forms of beauty, and though fancy may play (in some Plates) in extravagant variety, correctness and propriety are preserved. The scenes are so well selected, that the Plates will afford a connected view of the whole drama. The exact repetition of the same details of costume in every identical spot, for instance in Faust's study, and in Martha, and Margaret's chambers, makes us feel at home with them, and traces a sort of biography of the inmates; an effect similar to that which we find (even in our days) in the sitting-rooms of honest citizens in small towns of the German empire where the people are Roman Catholics. At Mother Martha's you see old-fashioned rubbish; in Margaret's chamber, cleanliness and female neatness are conspicuous in flower-pots and the spinning-wheel. Forty years ago, a doctor or chemist's study at Isny, Überkingen, or some other towns in that neighbourhood, very much resembled Faust's chamber; even Kästner's study was like it. The witch's kitchen and the scenery and figures of the Blocksberg, astonish us by their variety. In their monstrous extravagancies they will only excite a pleasant smile, not disgust. The simple means by which the most marked effect is produced, exhibits a striking coincidence of imagination with the poet and artist. Perhaps our fancy outstrips the artist's intention, when we conceive, for instance, the rock in Plate 21, on the left hand, to resemble a veiled woman.

The figures are drawn with similar propriety and expression. Margaret passes through the different gradations of reserve, maiden coyness, fondness, perplexity, yielding, ominous grief, wild repentance and utter despair. Faust changes from a monastic doctor to a gay knight; and his looks, gradually strained by the passions to the tension of despair, are conspicuous in the last Plate. Mephistopheles never appears as a bugbear, yet so much of a devil that we can always see how much the mask of decency struggles to fall off. The lappels of his cap are continually striving to change into horns; his goatish physiognomy would fain assume the features of a demon, but is never suffered: this character, however, gradually develops itself in his looks, as the scenes become more horrible. The true nature of the disgusting creature appears more and more as the scene maddens. At length, in the last Plate, his malice bursts forth and marks the furious destroyer.

We shall now proceed to the Analysis of the Book itself, without which the Plates would only stimulate without gratifying the appetite, and as the chief object of the Translator has been to preserve unimpaired, and to render as faithfully as possible the conceptions of the Author, it is hoped that any little inaccuracies of style will meet with the reader's kind indulgence.

A PRELUDE

On the Stage.

Enter.—*The Manager, the Dramatic Poet, and the Clown.*

The manager desires the poet to give him a medley full of action, with which the poet reluctantly complies, having more serious views; but the clown convinces him at last that all, even life itself, is a continual medley of vanity and folly. The manager requests the poet not to spare his scenery and machines, of which he has great store.

PROLOGUE.

The Scene is in Heaven.

Mephistopheles appears before the Deity, who is surrounded by angels and archangels praising his works—he complains that men torment themselves, and that they only use their reason to degrade themselves lower than the brute. He is asked whether he has nothing further to say? if he always comes to accuse? and if nothing can please him on earth? he answers, that he finds things are there, as ever, very wretched; he even pities man in his days of sorrow, and would fain desist from plaguing the wretched creature.—(Plate I. refers to this point.)

Mephistopheles then asks permission to tempt Faust whilst he lives on earth, which the Deity permits him to do, with this remark,—though he now serves me with distraction, I shall soon lead him to clearness: the gardener knows that when the young tree shoots, blossoms and fruit will sprout from it in a few years.

Engraved by Henry Moses

Published by Baldwyn & Sons, Bread Street June 1 1820.

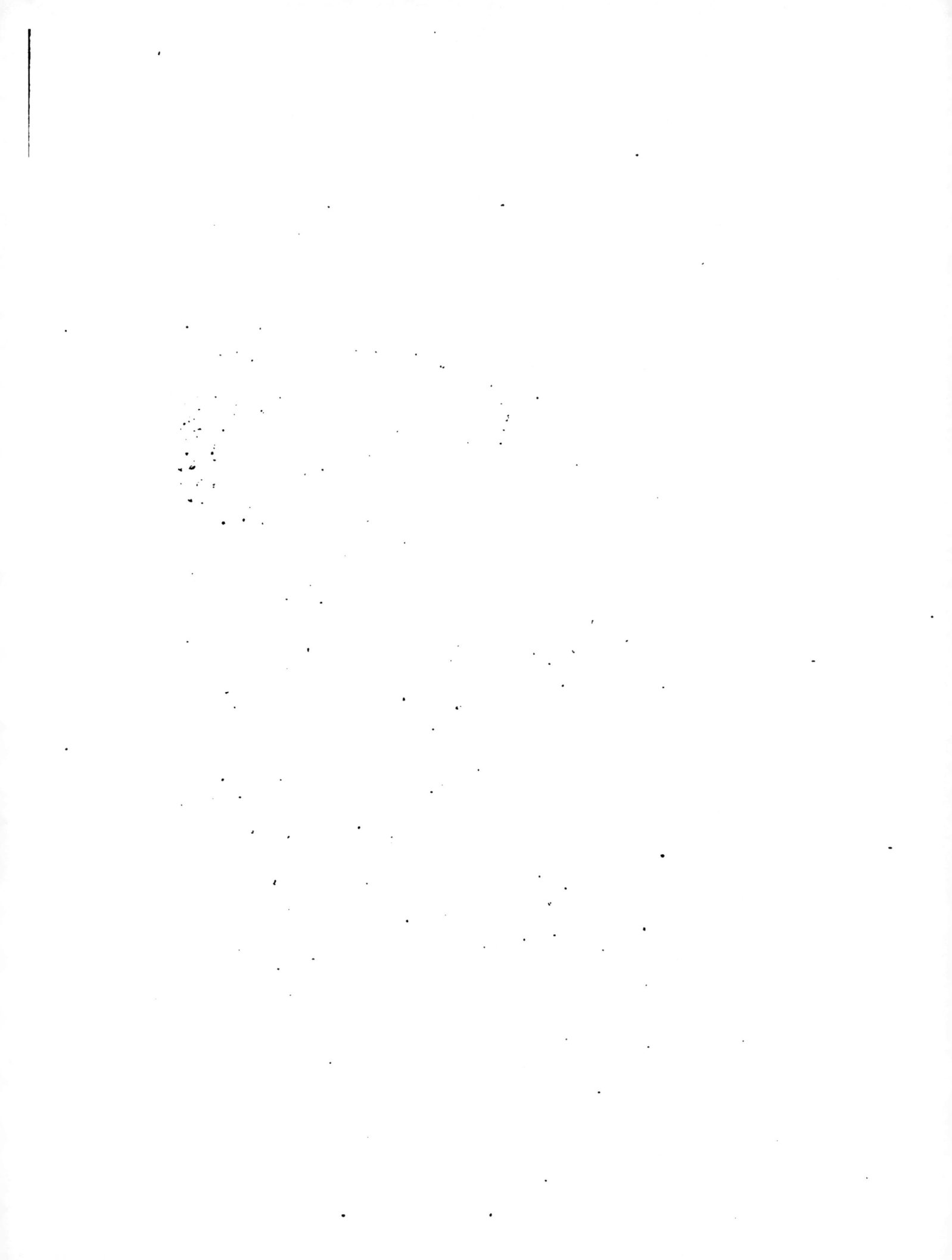

THE TRAGEDY.

FIRST PART.

The Scene,—Night. FAUST *is discovered in a narrow, gothic, high-vaulted chamber, restless in his arm-chair, at a desk.*

Faust laments that he has studied philosophy, law, medicine, and theology, with eager application ; and observes, that though they call him Doctor he is now but as wise as before; that he has been leading his disciples astray these ten years, and is now convinced that all human knowledge is vain. Though he is beyond all scruples and doubts, and fears neither hell nor the devil, he has lost all enjoyment, and is left in extreme penury. In this state of mind he devotes himself to magic, desirous to converse with spirits, that he may learn what holds the universe together, and pry into the inmost energies of nature. He wishes he could walk on the tops of the highest mountains in the light of the full moon, and hover in the company of spirits, round rocks and in caverns. He loathes his gloomy chamber, which is dimly lighted through stained glass, encumbered with books, a prey to dust and worms, and crouded with glasses, vials, boxes, instruments, and old-fashioned furniture. Instead of living nature, in which God created man, he is surrounded with smoke and dust, with skeletons and dead bones. He resolves to go into the open field with magical works, in the hand-writing of Nostradamus, there to trace the course of the stars, and to discover how one spirit converses with another. In vain does dry meditation expound the sacred characters ; he is convinced that spirits are near him ; he calls upon them to answer him, if they hear.

On opening the book, he views the character of the macrocosm with delight, desirous of unfolding the powers of nature, whose effects he beholds in those characters. He reads: " The world of spirits is not closed, thy own senses are closed, thy heart is dead. Go, disciple, bathe your earthy breast in the redness of the morning!"

Turning over a leaf he beholds the character of the spirit of the earth, and continues his soliloquy: " How very differently I feel affected by this character. Thou, spirit of the earth, art most closely allied to me; I feel my powers raised; I glow as with fresh wine; I feel courage to venture into the world, to bear the woes, the fortunes of the earth, to be tossed in the storm, yet not to tremble in the wreck. A cloud collects above me—the moon hides her light—the lamp grows dim!—the smoke ascends!—red rays of light flash about my head—a breath of air waves down from the arched vault and seizes me with tremor! I feel thou dost hover about me, desired spirit. Show thyself! Ah! how my heart beats! How all my senses ferment with sensations quite new! I feel all my heart yielded up to thee! Thou must! thou must! and though it should cost me my life!"
(He seizes the book, and mysteriously pronounces the character of the spirit. A red flame ascends; the spirit appears in the flame.)

Spirit. Who calls me?

Faust. (turning away his face.) Terrible vision!

The SPIRIT reproves FAUST for feeling so suddenly dismayed, after having powerfully attracted him, and goes on to tell Faust, that he is a spirit ever active, in life, in actions, in birth, in death; a sea continually agitated by successive motion, a glow of life; thus he works the rustling loom of time, and weaves the living garment of the Deity.

Faust now feels himself nearly related to *the Spirit*, who retorts, " Thou resemblest the spirit whom thou dost comprehend, but not to me!" and disappears.

Faust (with a sudden shivering) " Not to thee? To whom then ? I, the image of the Deity ! and not even resemble thee !"

His *Famulus,* or Attendant, knocks. *Faust* laments that he comes to interrupt his sublime visions.

Enter *Wagner* in a night-gown, and night-cap, bearing a lamp. *Faust* turns away his face in disgust.

Wagner. " Excuse me. I heard you declaiming ; probably you were reading some Greek tragedy ? I should like to learn something of this art, which is so effectual now-a-days. I have frequently been told in commendation of it, that an actor from the stage might teach a parson."

Faust. " Yes, if the parson be a stage-actor, as it will happen at times."

Wagner. " Penned up in our study, and scarcely seeing the world on a holiday, and then as through a perspective glass, and at a distance, how can we lead it by persuasive eloquence ? "

Faust. " If you do not feel it you will never attain it, except it spring from your own soul, and with original energy draw the hearts of all your hearers ; but you will never create a heart to join your's unless it proceeds from your own. Seek only honest gain. Be not a fool, attracting notice with the bells. Reason, like common sense, propounds itself without art. Pompous words, curled with the flourishes of human oratory, are unrefreshing, like foggy winds rustling through the dry leaves in autumn."

Wagner. " Art is long, and our life is short! How difficult is it to attain the means, by which we may ascend to the sources ! And before we get half way, poor creatures ! we may die."

Faust. " And is parchment the holy well, one draught of which quenches thirst for ever ? You gain no refreshment, unless it springs from your own soul."

8

Wagner. " But it is very pleasing to seize the spirit of the times, to see how wise men thought before us, and how gloriously far we have got."

Faust. " O, yes; as far as the stars! What you call the spirit of the times, is in fact men's own spirit, in which the times are reflected as in a mirror. A wretched sight—a tub of sweepings and a lumber-room, and at most some grand action of state, with excellent pragmatical maxims, fit for the mouth of puppets at a fair. But the night is far spent, we must break off our discourse."

Wagner departs reluctantly, after he has requested *Faust* to allow him some further conversation on the morrow (Easter Sunday).

Faust (alone) proceeds in his former strain of discontent, till he espies a vial of poison, which he takes down from the shelf, and hails it as the means to raise him to the etherial regions, to a new life of pure activity and to higher spheres as a man, no longer a worm confined to the earth.—*He puts the vial to his lips.*

Ringing of bells and singing in chorus, behind the scenes.

Chorus of Angels.

" Christ is risen!
Joy to mortals
Who were laden
With destructive and
Hereditary faults."

Faust. " What deep sounds, what clear notes, wrest the vial from my lips? Do ye, tinkling bells, already announce the first hour of the celebration of Easter? Does the choir sing that consoling hymn; that hymn which once resounded from the lips of angels at the dark grave, the pledge of a new covenant?"

Chorus of Women.

With spices the richest
We come to embalm him,
We his tried friends
In fine linen had wrapt him,
And here laid him low.
Alas! he is gone,
Christ is not here!

Chorus of Angels.

" Christ is risen!
Bless'd be his friends,
Who have now stood the test,
The heart-rending, but
Wholesome and practical
Trial of faith."

Faust. " I hear the message, but I want the faith! I dare not soar to those spheres whence the cheering tidings come. And yet, used from my childhood to this sound, it calls me back to life. Remembrance withholds me from the last, serious step. O! continue your sweet heavenly hymns! The tear starts; earth has me again!"
A Chorus of Disciples, and afterwards of Angels.

Scene, the Country about the Gates of the Town.

Several Mechanics walking and conversing on Easter Sunday.
Two Servant Maids walking together and talking of their lovers.
Two Students following them.
A Citizen's Daughter regrets that fine young men, who might frequent the best company, should run after those girls.
A Citizen complains of the new mayor, and grumbles.

c

A Beggar, singing, addresses the men and women passing, and begs alms.

Two other Citizens, talking of the war in Turkey.

An Old Woman speaks to the citizen's daughters, admiring their dress, and tells them, she could procure what they desire.

A Citizen's Daughter says to another, " Agatha, let us go! I take care not to walk with such witches; though she has shewn me my future lover on St. Andrew's eve."

The other replies, " that she was shewn her's in a chrystal, like a soldier, accompanied by several others, but has never yet been able to meet with him."

Soldiers talking of sieges and women.

Enter *Faust* and *Wagner*.

Countrymen under a tree, singing and dancing.

An old Countryman addresses Faust, commending the learned doctor for deigning to come amongst them, drinks to him, and offers the can to Faust, who accepts it and drinks to the health of the company, who draw round him, and drink to the health of the doctor, who visited and cured the sick along with his late father.

Faust walks on with *Wagner*, to a stone, where they intend to rest themselves. " On this stone," says Faust, " I used frequently to sit thoughtful and alone, rich in hope, firm in faith, praying and fasting. Now the applause of the crowd sounds to me like scorn. Neither myself nor my father deserve their praise. He was an honest man, an alchymist, and prepared medicines, the patients died, and nobody inquired who recovered.

" Happy is the man who has a ray of hope left, to emerge from this ocean of error! What we know not, is the very thing we need, and what we know, we cannot use. But let us not waste this hour in melancholy! See, how the evening-sun gilds the cottages, surrounded

FAUST AND WAGNER.

Engraved by Henry Moses

with verdure. It hastens away and promotes new life. Oh! had I wings to follow him and view the world beneath my feet!—" But, alas! corporeal wings cannot join those of the spirit."

Wagner prefers books and study.

Faust. " You are conscious of one instinct only. Oh! may you never be sensible of the other! In my breast, alas! reside two souls. The one attaches itself to the world with riveting organs ; the other forcibly raises itself from the dust to higher regions. Oh! if there be spirits in the air, which hover through the space, and rule between earth and heaven, descend and bear me away to a new varied life! Oh, had I but a magic mantle to carry me to distant countries, I would not exchange it for the royal purple !"

Wagner. " Do not call down that host of spirits, who fill the atmosphere like a stream, and prepare a thousand dangers for man, from all quarters. From the North they advance with tongues pointed like a dart; from the East they come drying-up, and feed on your lungs : when the South sends them from the desert, heat and fire crowd on your head : the West brings a swarm, which first refreshes, and then drowns you and the field with a flood. They are ready to hear and to obey; their pleasure is to deceive and hurt us.— Let us go home ; the dusk of the evening advances. Why do you stand and look astonished? What ails you? (Plate II.)

Faust. " See you yon black dog scouring over sowed fields and stubble ?"

Wagner. " I saw him long since ; it appeared of no consequence."

Faust. " Consider him well! What do you take him for ?"

Wagner. " For a poodle, who in his own way endeavours to trace his master."

Faust. " Do you mind how he hunts about us, approaching in a spiral line, and if I mistake not, fiery currents issue from his paws like trains."

Wagner. " I see nothing but a black poodle-dog; your eyes may deceive you."

Faust. " To me it appears that he draws magic snares round our feet. The circle grows narrow; he is near."

Wagner. " You see it is a dog, and no spectre. He snarls and doubts, wags his tail, just as other dogs do."

Faust. " Join our company! Come hither!"

Wagner. " A singular animal. When you stand still, he attends you; if you lose any thing, he will fetch it, and jump in the water after your stick."

Faust. " You are right; I see no symptoms of a spirit, it is all the effects of teaching."

Wagner. " He deserves your favour."

They enter the gate of the town.

Scene the Study.

Enter *Faust* with the *Dog.*

Faust. " Dark night awakens our better soul. The ferocious and wild passions rest in sleep. Charity and the love of God are now stirring."

" Lay down, dog! Do not run to and fro! Why do you snuffle at the threshold? Lay down behind the stove; here is my best cushion.— Be a welcome and a quiet guest."

" When the friendly lamp burns in our narrow cell, our bosom clears up, if the heart knows itself. Reason speaks again, and hope buds afresh; we long for the rivulets, for the springs of life."

" Dog, snarl not!—We are used that men scoff at things which they do not comprehend, that they grumble at good things which

FAUST IN HIS STUDY.

Engraved by Henry Moses

Published by Baldwin & Cradock, Paternoster Row, June 1, 18..

frequently are troublesome to them : would a dog snarl, threat, as they do ?"

Faust feels restless again ; he turns to the Greek New Testament, and attempts to translate the beginning of St. John's Gospel.

" Dog, cease your howling and barking, or begone ; the door is open.—What do I see?—My dog swells immensely !—Now he is like an hippotamus, with sparkling eyes and terrific face.—Oh, I have you safe. Solomon's key will do for such brood of hell.

(Spirit in the passage.) " A captive is within. Follow him not.— Can you help him? abandon him not, for he has done us many favours."

(Faust tries the magic spells of the spirits of the four elements against the beast, but to no purpose.) " Art thou a fugitive from hell? Then behold this character, which the black host must respect. (See Plate III.) It swells now with bristles, banished behind the stove; it dissolves into a mist. Do not ascend to the ceiling! Lay down at your master's feet. Await not the strongest charm of my art."

Mephistopheles, whilst the mist descends, advances from behind the stove, dressed as a travelling student. " Why this stir ? What do you want, Sir ?"

Faust. " So this was the dog's kernel! A travelling student? A laughable case."

Mephistopheles acknowledges that Faust has made him tremble.
Faust asks his name.
Mephistophelcs ridicules so futile a question from a philosopher who covets the essence of things.

Faust. " With such folks as you, the essence generally is known by the name, being plain enough, when we call you Beelzebub, Destroyer, Liar. Well, then, who art thou ?

Mephist. " A part of that power which always wills evil, yet ever produces good. I am the spirit who always denies; and that justly; for whatever is made, deserves to perish; therefore, it were better if nothing were made. Accordingly all which you call sin, destruction, or in one word, evil, is my proper element."

Faust. " You call yourself a part, yet stand before me whole?"

Mephist. " I speak modest truth; whilst man, that little world of folly, commonly conceits himself to be a whole. I am a part of that darkness which engendered light; proud light which flows from matter, and is intercepted by bodies: thus, I hope, it will not exist long, but will perish with materiality."

Faust. " Now I comprehend your noble functions. You can annihilate nothing en masse; you, therefore, attempt to do it in detail. To the ever-active, salutary, creative power, you oppose the clenched hand of a devil, which spitefully closes itself in vain! Commence a better trade, thou whimsical son of Chaos."

Mephist. " We'll really consider of it more another time. May I go now?"

Faust. Why do you ask permission? Now, that I have made your acquaintance, visit me in any way you like. Here is the window, there the door; or the chimney is likewise at your service."

Mephist. " I confess a trifling obstacle prevents my exit, the pentagon on your threshold."—

Faust. " How did you get in then?"

Mephist. " Examine it closely. It is not correctly drawn. One angle, that which faces the outside, has a little gap.—The *dog* did not perceive it, when he leaped in; but now the thing wears a different aspect; the *devil* cannot get out."

Faust. " But why do you not go out at the window?"

Mephist. " It is a law with devils and spectres, ' the way by which they enter, by that they must go out.' The former is optional, the latter is imperative on us."

Faust. " Even hell has its laws! I like the thing: then I suppose a covenant may be made with such gentry as you, and that safely?"

Mephist. " What we promise, you shall have, without any stinting deduction. But this is not to be done in a moment. I beg you to dimiss me for the present, I pray you.

Faust. " I have laid no trap for you. You fell into the snare of your own accord. When we have caught the devil, we should hold him fast; he is not easily caught a second time."

Mephist. " If you wish it, I am ready to remain ; but on condition that I may shew you my art, to pass the time away."

Faust. " With all my heart ; you may do so ; but let it be a pleasing art."

Mephist. desires the spirits to sing, and promises to gratify his sight, his smell, his taste and feeling.

Spirits sing and produce various sights, till Faust falls asleep.

Mephist. thanks them, and says that Faust is not knowing enough to detain the devil. He desires the spirits to keep him asleep by pleasant dreams. Then in his capacity as lord of rats and mice, flees, frogs, bugs, lice, &c. he calls a rat, and commands it to gnaw off the fatal angle of the pentagon, which he sprinkles with oil. This is done, and he is off.

Faust awakes, and finds that he is cheated; fancies the devil had appeared to him in a dream, and that the dog has run away.

* * *

Scene, the Study.

Faust. " Some one knocks. Come in !"

Mephistopheles enters dressed as a noble squire, in a red suit, embroidered with a silk mantle, in his hat a cock's feather, a long, narrow sword by his side. He advises Faust to dress himself like him, in order to be disengaged and free, and to enjoy life.

Faust. " In any garb I shall feel the torments of this confined life on earth. I am too old merely to play, too young to be without desires. What gratification can the world afford me? Existence is a burden to me, my life is hateful."

Mephist. " And yet death is never a welcome guest."

Faust. " O! blessed is the man, around whose temple death winds the blood-stained wreath of laurel in the glory of victory; the man, whom Death finds after a merry dance in the arms of his beloved. Oh! had I but dropt down unsouled, in raptures before the energies of the supreme spirit!"

Mephist. " And yet I know a certain person who would not drink a brown mixture the other night."

Faust. " It seems you are fond of watching our actions."

Mephist. " I am not omniscient; but I know many things."

Faust. " Though a sweet and well-known tune snatched me from the dreadful conflict of thoughts, and by the recollection of blissful days deceived the remnant of youthful sensations; I now curse whatever captivates the soul with lures and juggling, and binds it in this den of grief by delusive, false, and flattering spells! Cursed be the high opinion of conceit in which the mind inwraps itself! Cursed be the delusion of the phenomena, which attach themselves to our senses! Cursed be our hypocritical dreams of fame, the deception of our lasting name! Cursed whatever flatters us under the specious denomination of possessions, such as a wife and child, a servant and a plough! Cursed be Mammon, when he excites us to bold actions by treasure, when he lays us a pillow for idle enjoyment! Cursed be the balmy virtue of the grape! A curse to the greatest kindness of love! A curse to hope! A curse to faith! and above all things, a curse to patience!"

Chorus of invisible Spirits.

Woe! woe!
Thou hast destroy'd it,
That charming world ;
At thy potent stroke,
It falls in pieces !
A demi-god has destroy'd it !
We shall carry
The fragments off to naught,
And bewail
The loss of that beauty.
Powerful
Son of the earth, oh !
Build it again,
In your own bosom rear it up !
Commence thou
A new course of life
With clear sensations,
And then new hymns will
Anon resound !

Mephistopheles. " These are the little ones of my own crew. Hear what sage advice they give for enjoyment and action. They want to entice you to quit your solitude, in which the senses and juices are stagnated.

" Cease to indulge your grief, which preys upon your life like a vulture. The worst company will make you sensible that you are a man amongst men. If you will go through life in my company, I will submit to be yours directly. I am your companion, and if it suits you, I am your servant, your slave !"

Faust. " And what shall I perform for you in return ?"

Mephist. " You have a long time granted for that."

Faust. " No, no! The devil is selfish, and does not grant favours for nothing. Speak out, and state your terms distinctly; such a servant is dangerous."

Mephist. " I will engage to serve you *here*; I will neither flinch from, nor be idle in your service: when we meet again *yonder*, you shall do the like for me."

Faust. " I care little for *yonder* world. When you have first dashed this world to atoms, the other may arise afterwards. My joys spring from this earth, and it is this sun which shines on my sufferings: when I can separate from them, then let happen what will and may. Whether they hate and love in the future state, and whether there be something above and below in yonder spheres, of such things I will not hear another word."

Mephist. " Being in this mind, you may venture. Engage yourself; and you shall see my arts and rejoice; I'll give you what no man ever saw."

Faust. " Poor devil! what can you give? Was ever the spirit of a man in his aspiring tension, comprehended by any such as you? But you have got food which does not satisfy hunger; you have got yellow gold, which never enduring, separates in your hand like quicksilver; a game, at which we never win; a girl, who, reclining in my bosom, engages with a neighbour by ogling; the godlike enjoyment of honour, which vanishes like a meteor. Shew me the fruit which rots ere it be pluck'd, and trees which daily sprout fresh verdure!"

Mephist. " Such orders do not frighten me; I can procure you such treasures. But, my friend, the time approaches when we wish to enjoy good fare in quiet ease."

Faust. " If ever I lie down satisfied on a bed of sloth, then may it be my ruin! If by flattery you can ever deceive me, so that I should be pleased with myself; if you can cheat me with enjoyment, let that be my last day! This will I wager!"

Mephist. " Done!"

Faust. " And done! If I should ever say to the fleeting moment, pray, tarry! thou art charming! then may you lock me in fetters;

FAUST MAKES OVER HIS SOUL TO MEPHISTOPHELES.

Published by Fisher, Son & Co., Newgate Street, London 1834

then am I willing to perish; then the knell of death may toll; then shall you be free from your service; the clock may stand, its hand may drop; time shall be over with respect to me!"

Mephist. " Consider it well, we shall not forget it."

Faust. " And you are fully entitled; I have not ventured rashly. As I go on, I am a slave : whether yours, or whose, I care not."

Mephist. " I shall perform my duty forthwith, this very day, at the doctor's feast. Only this!---As life and death are uncertain, I request a few lines." (See Plate IV.)

Faust. " You want a written voucher, fool! Did you never know a man, and the word of a man? Is it not enough, that my given word shall decide my fate for ever? Does not the world rave madly on like a rushing torrent, and shall I be bound by a promise? But this persuasion is rooted in our heart. Happy is the man who carries faith in his pure bosom ; he will regret no sacrifice! But a piece of parchment with hand and seal is a bugbear which all men shun. The word dies away in the pen, the wax and skin alone retain the bond. What dost thou want of me, Evil Spirit? Brass, marble, parchment, or paper? Shall I write with a graver, a chisel, or a pen? I give you the choice."

Mephist. " How you inflate your oratory in the heat of temper! Any slip of paper will do. Sign your name with a little drop of blood."

Faust. " If this fully satisfies you, I'll comply with the silly whim."

Mephist. " Blood is a very peculiar juice."

Faust. " Fear not that I should break this covenant! To aspire with all my energy is exactly what I promise. I was inflated with too much vanity; I belong only to thy rank of beings. The great spirit has slighted me; nature locks herself up from me. The thread of meditation is broken; I have nauseated all knowledge long since. Let us assuage the glowing passions in the depths of sensuality! Let every wonder be instantly ready, enveloped in impenetrable magic

Let us plunge into the rustling stream of time, into the rolling course of events! There let pain and enjoyment, let success and mortification, alternately succeed as they can. A man acts restlessly."

Mephist. " No measure or term is placed to you. Boldly lay hold of pleasure, and be not bashful."

Faust. " Pleasure is not what I want. I devote myself to folly---to painful enjoyment---to hatred in love---to gratifying vexation. My bosom, cured of all thirst after knowledge, shall henceforth be open to all grief, and that which is allotted to the whole human race I wish to taste in my inmost self, to heap its weal and its woe upon my breast, and thus expand my own self into its whole essence, and, like the human race, at length go to wreck myself."

Mephist. " O, believe me, who many thousand years have chewed this hard food, from the cradle to the bier no man digests the old leaven! Believe me, the universe was only made for a God! He dwells in eternal splendour; us has he sent into darkness; and for you day and night are the only things suitable."

Faust. " But I will!"

Mephist. " Well, then, only one thing I fear; time is short, art is long. Let me instruct you. Associate with some poet; let him rove with his fancy, and heap all noble qualities upon your honoured *front*, the lion's courage, the stag's swiftness, the Italian's fiery blood, the long life of the Norwegian; let him find out for you the secret of combining generosity with craft, and of falling in love with the ardour of youth upon fixed rules. I should like to know such a person myself, and would call him Mr. Microcosm."

Faust. " But what am I? If it be impossible to obtain the crown of human nature, for which all sensations strive."

Mephist. " You are, after all---what you really are. Though you should wear a wig with a million of curls, and raise your feet on buskins a yard high, you will always remain what you are."

Faust. " I feel it; in vain have I scraped together all the treasures of the human intellect; yet when I sit down after all, no new energy stirs within me; I am not a hair's-breadth higher, not nearer to the infinite.

Mephist. " We must be wiser before the joys of life flee from us. Surely hands, feet, head, and every other part are yours; but because I enjoy every new thing, is it less mine on that account? When I can keep six steeds, is not their strength mine? I run as if I had twenty-four legs. Courage, then! leave off thinking, and fly forward through the world with me! I tell you, a speculative fellow is like a beast led about by an evil spirit in a circle on a barren heath, surrounded by the finest and most verdant pastures."

Faust. " How shall we set about it?"

Mephist. " We'll go out. Let your neighbour Paunch tire himself and the boys. Why would you be plagued to thrash straw? The best of what you know, you dare not tell the lads. There, I hear some one coming in the passage."

Faust. " It is impossible for me to see him now."

Mephist. " The poor lad has been waiting a long while; he must not go unrelieved. Come, lend me your gown and cap; the masquerade will make me look nobly."

(He changes his dress.)

" Now leave it to my wit. I want only a quarter of an hour. In the meanwhile prepare yourself for the delightful journey."

[*Exit* FAUST.

Mephist. (in Faust's long gown.) " Now, then, despise reason and science, the sublimest energies of man: may the lying spirit confirm you in delusion, and in the practice of magic, and I have you unconditionally! Fate has given him a mind which with unbridled ardour ever presses forward, and whose over-eager effort overleaps the pleasures of the world. I'll drag him through a roving life of tame insignificance; I'll make him sprawl, stare, stick fast, and his insatiate appetite shall be ministered to with meat and drink; he will long in vain for refreshment, and though he had not sold himself to the devil, still must he go to ruin!"

A Disciple enters, who requests the sham doctor to instruct him, as he is desirous of becoming a great scholar.

Mephist. advises him to improve his time by a regular method; first to frequent the lectures on logic, where his mind will be well drilled, and laced up in Spanish boots, in order to creep on at a fair rate, and not to flit, like a " *will-o'-the-wisp,*" backwards and forwards. Afterwards he should learn metaphysics, taking lessons five hours every day; and writing down what he learns. After a witty review of the learned faculties (or professions of law, divinity, and physic), the Disciple presents his album to Mephistopheles, and desires him to write a line in it for a keepsake.

Mephistopheles writes, and the *Disciple* reads as follows:

": *Eritis sicut deus, scientes bonum et malum.* The Disciple puts up the book very respectfully and retires.

Mephist. " Only follow the old adage and my aunt, the serpent, and you will surely one day rue your likeness to the gods!"

Faust (entering). " Whither shall we go now?"

Mephist. " Where you please. We'll see the lesser, next the greater world."

Faust. " I never could conform myself to the world with my long beard, and shall always be at a loss."

Mephist. " Pooh! You will soon learn the way. The moment you assume an air of self-confidence you possess manners."

Faust. " How shall we travel? Where are your horses, carriage, and coachmen?"

Meph. " We need only spread your mantle; it will carry us through the air. Only take no large bundle with you. A little gas, which I shall prepare, will lift us up from the earth, and if we are light, we shall ascend quickly. I congratulate you on your new course of life.

Scene, Auerbach's Cellar in Leipzig.

Merry fellows drinking.

Frosch, Brander, Siebel, and *Altmayer* conversing, drinking and singing alternately. They pass some low jokes, and, amongst other things, talk of electing a Pope, who must possess a decisive quality, to exalt the man.---(A chaste allusion to the *sella stercoraria.)*

Enter FAUST *and* MEPHISTOPHELES.

Mephist. " I must first introduce you to merry company, that you may see how easy it is to live. These good people enjoy a feast every day. With little wit and much self-complacency each of them turns in a narrow circle, like kittens hunting their own tail. As long as they do not complain of the head-ache, and the host gives them credit, they are happy and free from care."

Brander. " They are travellers; I can see it by their odd manners."

Siebel. " For what do you take the strangers?"

Frosch. " Let me alone! I'll manage them with a full glass. They seem to be noblemen; they look proud and discontented.

Brander. " I'll lay a wager they are mountebanks."

Altmayer. " Perhaps so."

Frosch. " Mind how I shall quiz them."

Mephistopheles to Faust. " These fellows would never smell the devil, were he even to seize them by the collar."

Faust compliments them.

Siebel returns the compliment, and casting a side glance at Mephistopheles, says *(aside),* " Does that fellow halt with one leg?"

Frosch. " I dare say you set off late from Rippach?   Did you sup first with Jack Ketch?"

Mephist. " We quitted him to-day.   We had some conversation with him lately.   He talked much of his cousins, and begged to be remembered to every one of them."---*(He bows to Frosch.)*

Altmayer (aside). " There's for you! He is the sort."

Siebel. " A sly chap!"

After some further conversation (in which Faust bears no part) and a song by *Mephistopheles*, the latter says that he would be glad to drink to the success of reform, if their wine were better.   He offers to give them some from his cellar, if the host would not be angry."

Siebel takes upon him to answer for the host, and desires to have some of it.

Mephist. takes a gimblet out of a basket of tools belonging to the house, and asks each person what wine he desires to have.

They each of them choose, apparently much surprised.

Mephistopheles bores a hole in the edge of the table where Frosch sits, and asks for a bit of bees'-wax to use for corks, which is produced and made into stoppers by one of the company, whilst *Mephistopheles* bores holes towards each person of the company.   They think he is jeering them, or playing juggler's tricks, but he assures them to the contrary."

When all the holes are bored and stopped up,

Mephist. (with strange gestures,)

> " The vine bears grapes!
> The goat has horns;
> Wine is juice, but the vine is wood,
> The table of wood, can also yield wine.
> Here see deeper into nature!
> This is a miracle, only believe it:
> Now quickly draw your corks and drink!"

(See Plate V.) they draw the corks: the wine which each had chosen runs immediately into their glasses.

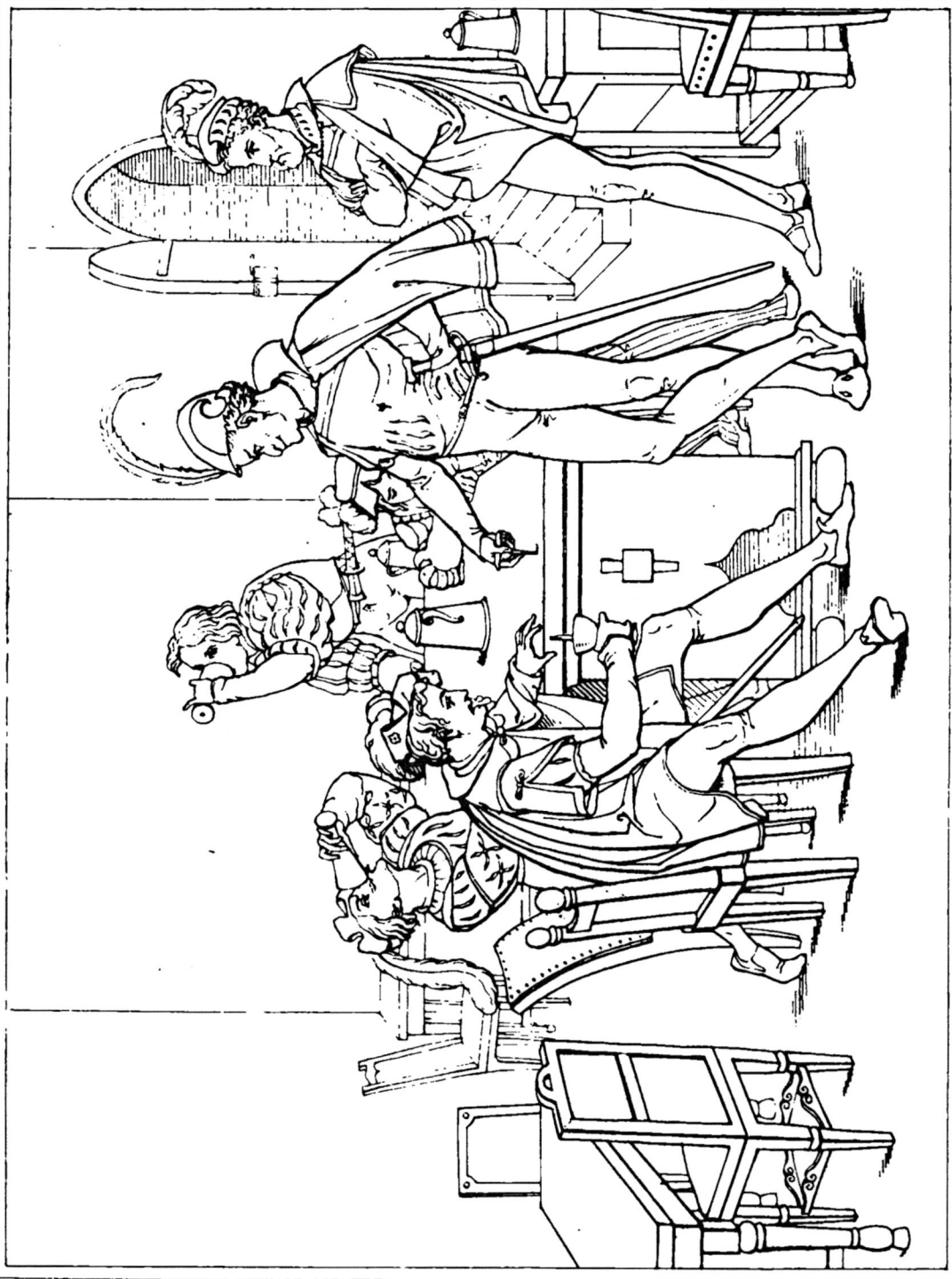

FAUST AND MEPHISTOPHELES IN THE TAVERN.

" O! the choice fountain which yields our fill!"

Mephist. " But only take care you do not spill."

They drink repeatedly.

All singing. " We feel a savage joy, just as five hundred swine would."

Faust wishes to go, but *Mephistopheles* desires him to stop and see the glorious effects of their beastliness.

Siebel drinks carelessly; the wine flows on the floor, and turns into a flame.—" Help! Fire! Help! It burns like hell!"

Mephist. setting a spell upon the flame. " Be quiet, friendly element."

To Siebel.

" For this time it was only a drop of purgatory."

The company quarrel with Mephistopheles; *Altmayer* draws a cork from the table, and the fire flies in his face.

Altmayer. " I burn! I burn!"

Siebel. " Witchcraft! At him! That fellow is outlawed!"

They draw their knives, and advance upon Mephistopheles.

Mephistopheles with a serious look,

> " False vision and face
> Change sense and place!
> Be here and be there!"

They stand astonished, and look at each other.

Altmayer. " Where am I? What a fine country!"

Frosch. " Vineyards! Do I see clearly?"

Siebel. " And grapes close at hand!"

Brander. " Under this green arbour, see what a vine! see what a grape!"

He takes Siebel by the nose. The others do the same reciprocally, and brandish their knives.

E

Mephist. as before. " Delusion; let go the spell which binds their eyes! And remember how the devil sports with you."

He disappears with Faust; the company quit hold of each other.

Siebel. " What now?"

Altmayer. " How?"

Frosch. " Was that your nose?"

Brander (to Siebel). " And I have got hold of yours."

Siebel. " Where is that fellow? If I catch him, he shall not get off alive.

Altmayer. " I saw him getting out at 'the cellar-door, riding on a cask.—My legs are as heavy as lead. *(Turning to the table.)* Will the wine flow again?"

Siebel. " It was all delusion and trick."

Frosch. " Yet I thought I drank wine."

Brander. " But what became of the grapes?"

Scene, a Witch's Cavern.

On a low hearth a large caldron stands over the fire. Various figures appear in the steam which ascends from it. A FEMALE MONKEY *sits by the caldron, and skims it, taking care that it does not boil over.* THE MALE MONKEY *and the young ones sit by the fire, warming themselves. The strange and fantastic furniture of a witch ornament the sides and roof.*

Enter *Faust* and *Mephistopheles.*

Faust. " I am sick of these mad tricks of magic. Do you promise me I shall recover from this farrago of madness? Am I now to ask advice of an old woman? And will that filthy mess make me thirty years younger? Woe is me, if you know nothing better. My hope is gone already. Has nature, and has a noble spirit discovered nothing better?"

Mephist. " My friend, now you talk wisely again. Yet there is also a natural means to make you young; but it is written in a different book, and is a strange chapter."

Faust. " I must know it."

Mephist. " Well! A means, to be had without money, without physician and witchcraft. Go to the field; set about hoeing and digging; feed on simple fare; live with cattle like a beast; and manure the soil which you reap yourself. This is the best means, I assure you, to make you young for eighty years to come."

Faust. " I am not used to that; I cannot submit to take a spade in my hand; I do not like to lead a confined life."

Mephist. " Then we must apply to the witch."

Faust. " What, to the old woman? Can you not brew the beverage yourself?"

Mephist. " A pretty pastime for me, forsooth! I could build a thousand bridges in the time required for such a tedious work. It takes many years to ferment well, and the ingredients are very strange. Though the devil has taught her, yet the devil cannot make it."

To the Animals.

" It seems your mistress is not at home."

The Animals. " At a feast; from home; gone up the chimney."

Mephist. " What are you stewing?"

Animals. " Beggars' broth."

Meph. " Then you have a numerous public."

The male monkey approaches Mephistopheles fawning. " O throw the dice and make me rich, and let me win! I am badly off, but had I money, I should be in my senses.

Mephist. " How happy would the monkey be, could he put in the lottery !"

In the meanwhile the young monkeys play with a large earthenware globe, and roll it about.

The male monkey. " That is the world ; it rises and falls, and rolls continually ; it rings like glass, and how brittle it is ! 'Tis hollow within.   Take this fire-screen, and sit down in the arm-chair !"

Faust. Standing before a mirror, alternately approaching and receding from it. " What do I see? What a heavenly figure appears in this magic mirror O Love ! lend me your swiftest wings and bear me to her ! Ah, when I venture to go near, I can only see her as in a mist.— There is nothing to equal her on earth."

Mephist. " I know where to find such a one for you.   For the present, look your fill."

Faust continues to look in the glass.   Mephistopheles stretching his limbs in the arm-chair, and playing with the screen, proceeds :

" Here I sit like a king on his throne ; I hold the sceptre, but not the crown.   (See Plate VI.)

The Animals having made many odd gestures, bring a crown to Mephistopheles with great shouts. They handle it awkwardly, it falls, and breaks into two pieces, with which they dance about.

Faust. facing the mirror. " Alas ! I am almost distracted.

Mephist. (Pointing to the animals.) " My head is almost ready to turn."

The cauldron being neglected by the female monkey, boils over ; a great flame ascends the chimney. *The witch* descends through the flame, with dreadful screams. *Mephistopheles* makes himself known to her ; she wonders he has not a cloven foot; but he tells her, that refinement has extended even to the devil, who no longer displays his horns, tail, and claws ; and as to that foot, which is indispensable,

PL. 6.

FAUST AND MEPHISTOPHELES IN "THE WITCHES CAVE.

THE WITCH GIVES FAUST THE MAGIC POTION.

as it would prejudice people against him, he, like many young men, wears false calves to his legs.

The witch dancing.—" I almost lose my senses at seeing Squire Satan once more with me !"

Mephist. " That name, woman, I hate !"

Witch. " Why so? What harm did it do you?"

Mephist. " It is set down in the book of fables long since; but men do not fare a whit the better on that account; they have got rid of *the evil one ; the evil ones* continue amongst them. Now give us a glass of that well-known liquor ! But of the oldest, for age doubles its strength."

Witch. " With all my heart. Here is a bottle of which I sometimes drink myself, and which does not stink at all; I'll give you a glass of it with pleasure. *(Aside to Mephistopheles.)* But if that gentleman drinks it unprepared, you know he cannot live an hour."

Mephist. " He is a good friend, to whom it will be of service. Draw your circle, and give him a cup full."

The witch, with strange gestures, describes a circle, and places a number of whimsical things in it: the glasses begin to ring, the cauldrons to resound, making music. At length she fetches a large book, and places the monkeys in the circle, who serve her for a desk, and to bear the torch. She beckons *Faust* to step to her; *Mephistopheles* invites *Faust* to walk into the circle. *The witch* reads and emphatically declaims some nonsensical stuff from the book, and thereupon, with many ceremonies, pours the draught into a cup. As *Faust* is putting it to his lips, a slight flame issues from it. (See Plate VII.)

Mephist. " Drink it up boldly ! Courage ! Thou intimate with the devil, and wouldst shrink from a flame !"

Faust steps out of the circle, and the witch destroys it.

Mephist. " Now let us walk ! You must not stand still.—You must absolutely perspire."

Faust. " Let me look in the mirror once more !"

Mephist. " No ! No ! You shall soon see the paragon of all wo-men actually before you. *(aside.)* With this draught in your body, you will see a Helen in every woman."

Scene.   *A Street.*   (See Plate VIII.)

FAUST.—MARGARET *passing by.*

Faust. " My fair lady, may I venture to offer you my arm and company ?"

Margaret. " I am neither a lady nor fair ; I can walk home by myself." She disengages herself and walks off.

Faust. " By heavens, this girl is beautiful ! I never saw her equal. She is so modest and virtuous, though at the same time a little pert. Her red lips, her blooming cheeks, I shall never forget them ! How she casts down her eyes ! it is deeply imprinted in my heart : and how quick she was with a smart answer : why, this is quite delightful !"

Enter MEPHISTOPHELES.

Faust. " Hear me, you must get me that girl !"

Mephist. " Which ?"

Faust. " She who passed by just now."

Mephist. " What, her ? She came from her priest, who has absolved her from all her sins : she is quite an innocent creature, who went to confess what she had never committed. I have no power over her !"

Faust. " But she is past fourteen. And if she rest not in my arms this night, you and I shall part at midnight."

Pl. 8

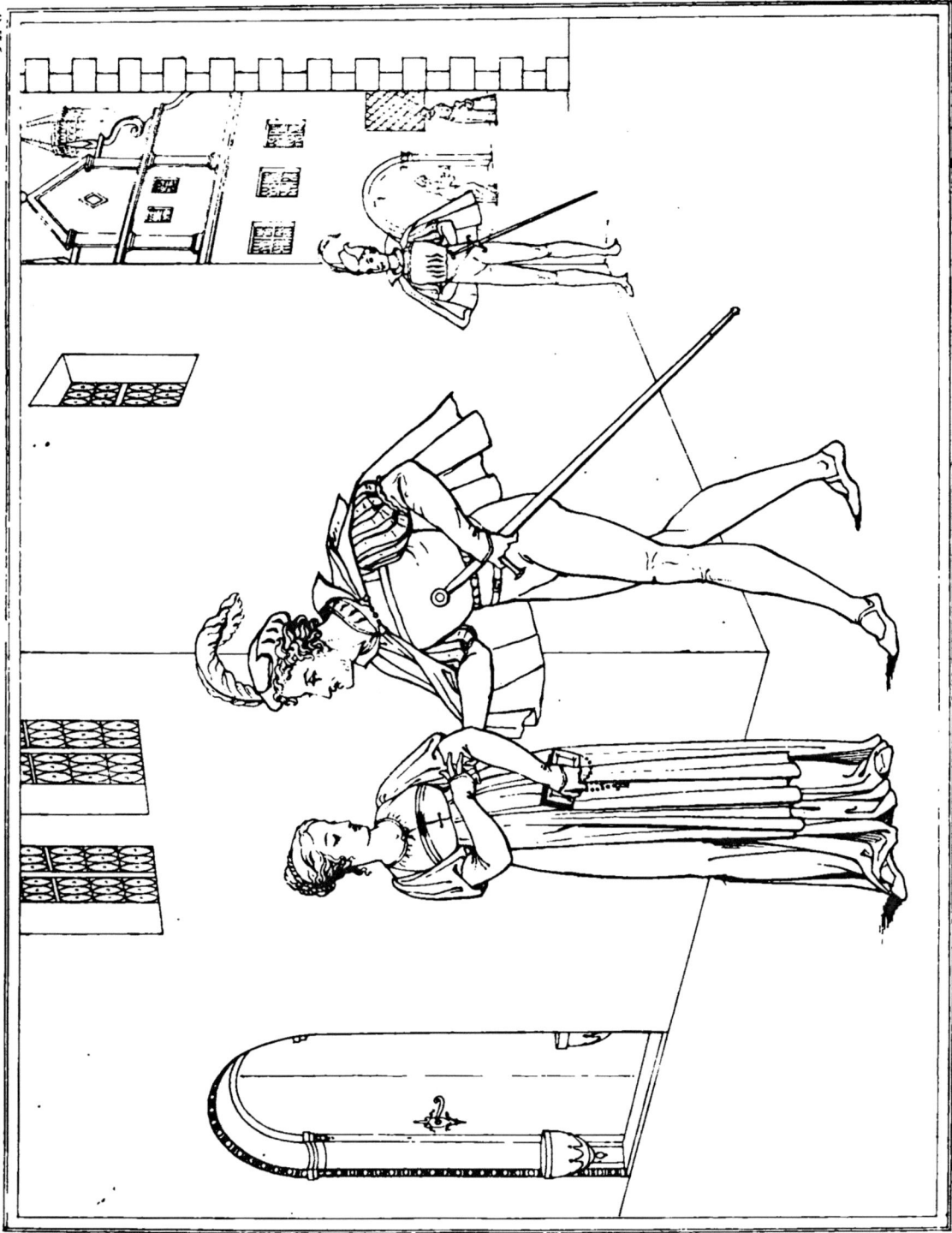

FAUST SEES MARGARET FOR THE FIRST TIME.

Engraved by Henry Moses.

Published by Boosey & Sons 4. Broad Street. June 1 1821.

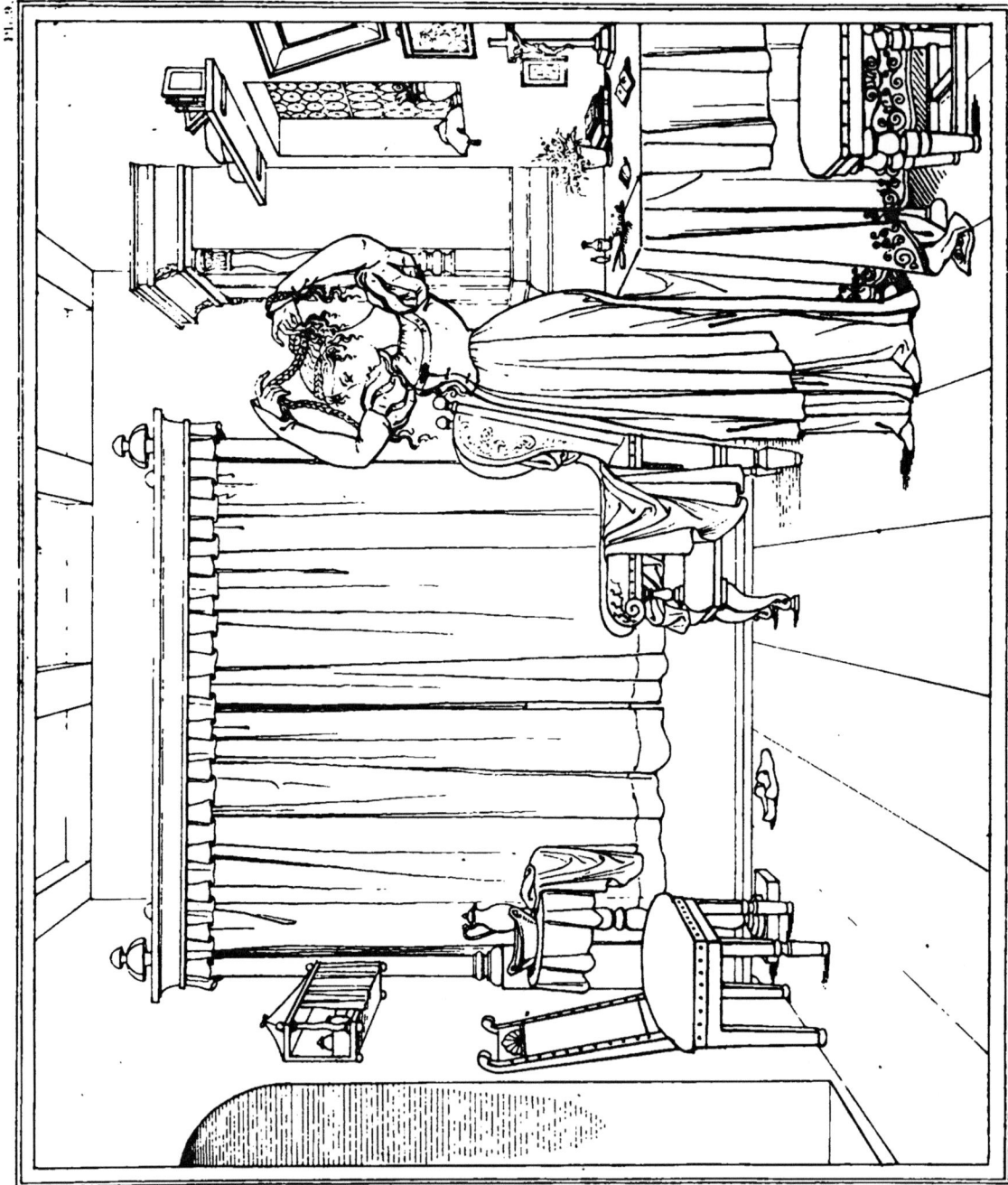

MARGARET IN HER CHAMBER.

Engraved by Henry Moses

Published by Henry Moses, 4 Broad Street June 1825

Mephistopheles tells him that it will take at least fourteen days merely to find an opportunity.

Faust. " Had I but seven hours leisure, I should not want the devil's assistance to seduce that innocent creature."

Mephist. " We cannot take her by force ; we must use cunning."

Faust. " Get me something from that angel ! Take me to her bed-chamber ! Get me a handkerchief from her breast ! Any thing belonging to her !

Mephistopheles promises to take him to her chamber that very day.

Faust. " Procure me a present for her." [*Exit.*

Mephist. " To make a present directly ? That is well done ! Now he will succeed ! I know many places and many buried treasures ; I must look round a little." [*Exit.*

EVENING.

A small neat chamber.

Margaret platting and tying up her hair. (See Plate IX.) " I would give any money to know who that gentleman was whom I saw to-day. He certainly looked very handsome. I could read in his looks that he is of noble family, or he would not have been so presuming. [*Exit.*

Enter MEPHISTOPHELES and FAUST.

Mephist. " Come in softly, come in !

Faust. (*after a short pause.*) " Pray leave me alone."

Mephist. (*prying about.*) " Not many girls are so neat." [*Exit.*

Faust. (*looking round him.*) " Hail, thou sweet twilight which prevailest in this sanctuary. Seize my heart, thou sweet pang of love, which longing, livest on the dew of hope. How all around breathes an air of repose, of order, of content! what riches in this poverty! In this prison what happiness!"

He throws himself down in the leathern arm-chair by the bed-side. (See Plate X.)

" Receive me! thou, who in joy and grief hast received her ancestors with open arms! How many children have often clung around this paternal throne! Here, perhaps, my lovely girl, with the plump cheeks of childhood, grateful for a Christmas gift, has piously kissed the withered hand of her grandfather. I feel, dear girl! thy spirit of competence and order breathe around me!—And here—(*He raises one of the bed-curtains.*)—What a fluttering of joy seizes me! Here I could tarry for hours. Nature! here in light dreams thou didst perfect the inborn angel."

" And thou! what brought thee here?—Why does thy heart feel oppressed? Faust, pitiful wretch! I no longer know thee. I feel melting in a dream of love! Are we the sport of every pressure of the air?—And should she enter this moment, how should I be punished for my presumption! The great man, ah how little! would fall enraptured at her feet."

Mephist. " Be quick! I see her coming below."

Faust. " Begone! I will never leave!"

Mephist. shews him a little box of presents, which he places in a cupboard, and closes the lock again, advising Faust to go. They depart.

Margaret enters, carrying a lamp. " It is so close here." She opens the window. " And yet it is not warm without. I feel, I know not how—I wish my mother had come home. A shivering runs all over my body—What a foolish, fearful girl I am!"

She sings a ballad, whilst she undresses herself. She opens the cupboard to put in her cloaths, and finds the casket of jewellery.

" How did this pretty box come here? I am sure I locked the cup-

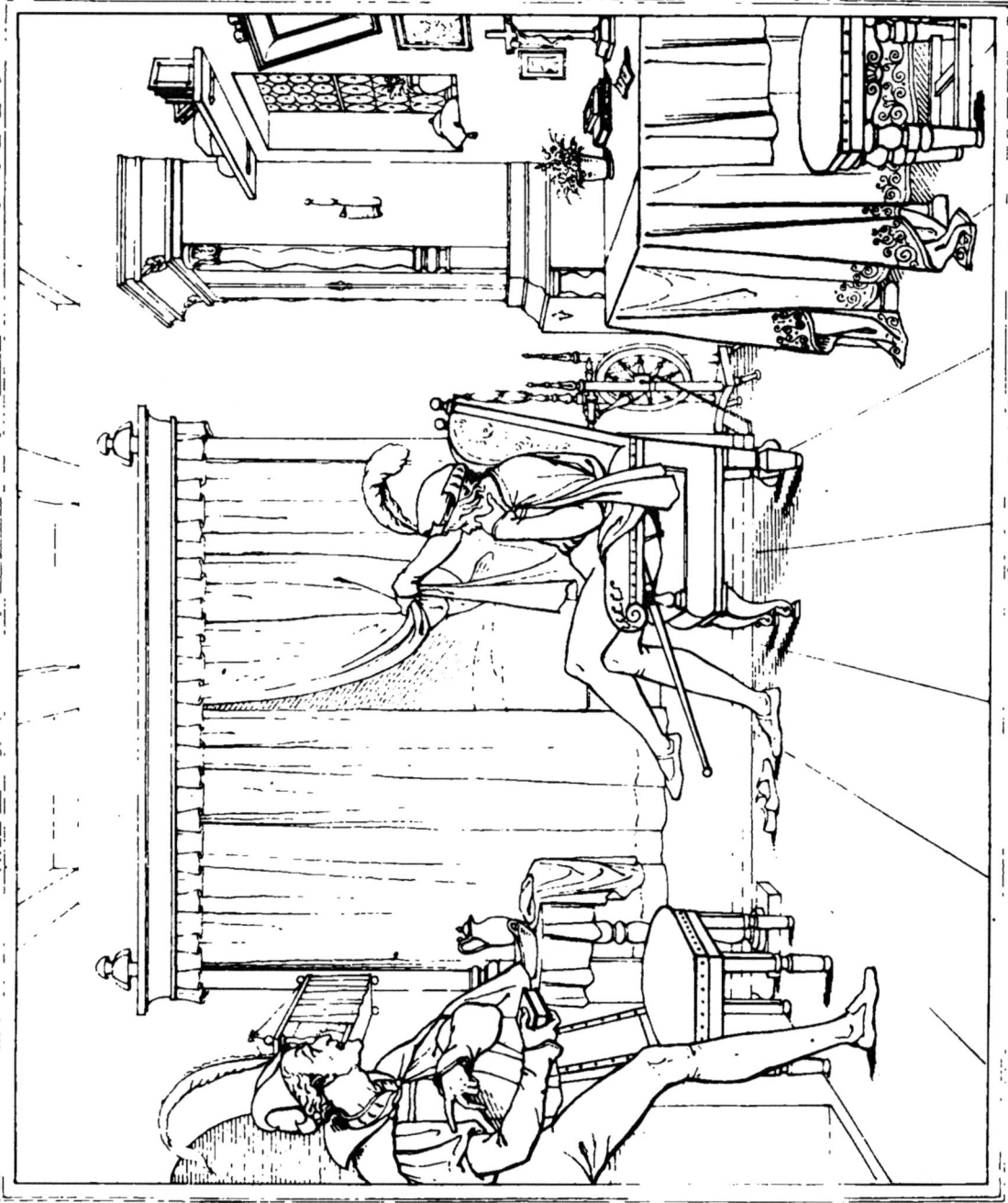

FAUST INTRODUCED INTO MARGARET'S CHAMBER BY MEPHISTOPHELES.

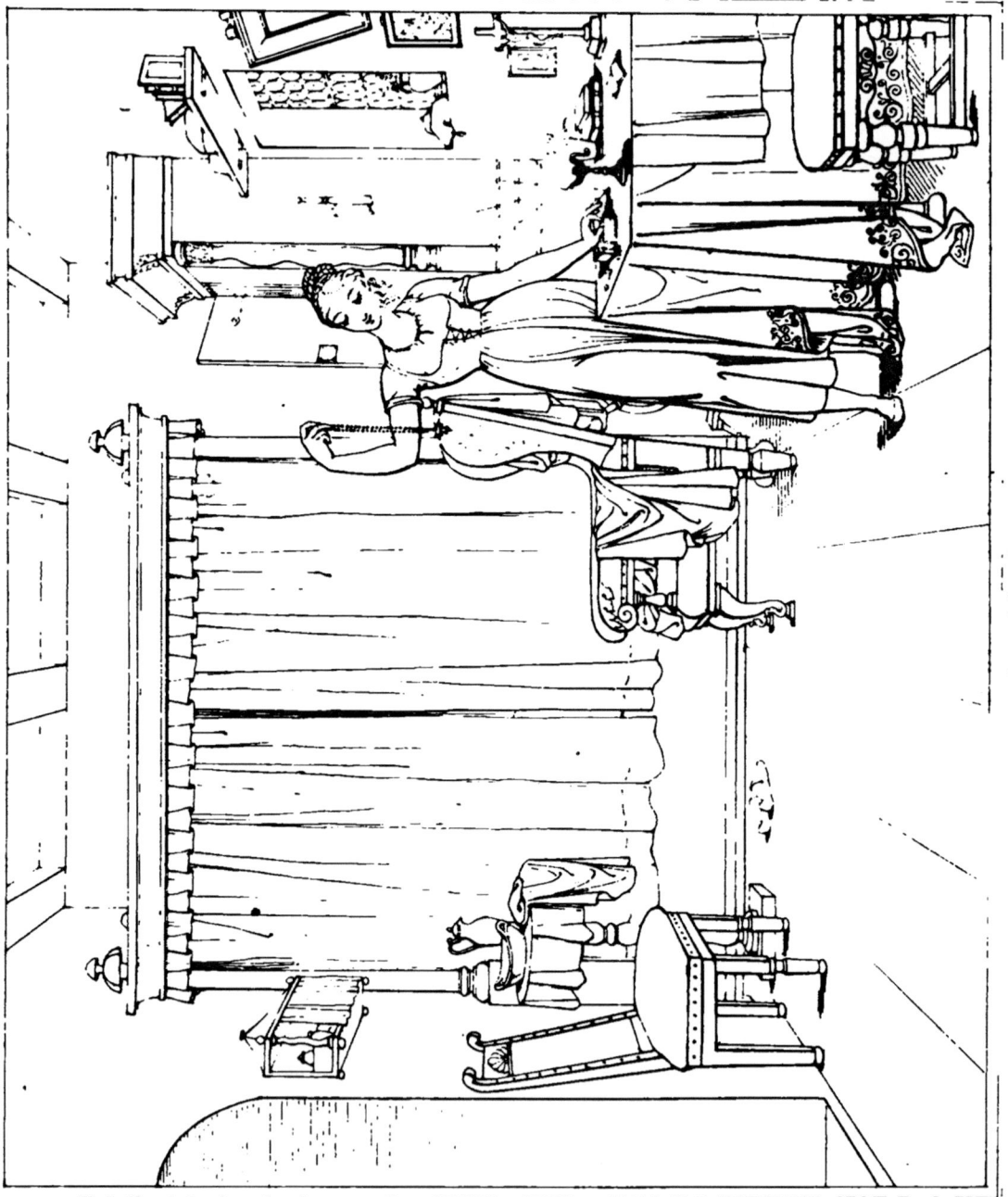

MEPHISTOPHELES LEAVES RICH ORNAMENTS IN MARGARET'S CHAMBER.

33

board. Tis very strange! What can it be? Perhaps some person left it as a pledge, and my mother has lent money on it. There is a small key tied to it; I think I will open it. What is that? I never saw any thing like it! Jewellery! A noble lady might wear these things on the greatest holiday. How will this chain fit me? To whom can these precious things belong?"

She decorates herself with them, and steps before the looking-glass. (See Plate XI.)

" I wish these ear-rings only were mine! I look much better with them on. What avails beauty, young girls? It is very well, but that is all. They praise you with a mixture of pity. Every person longs for gold; every thing depends upon it. Alas, we poor creatures!

A Public Walk.

Faust walking up and down, thoughtful.

Mephistopheles advancing to him. " By all slighted love! by the hellish element! I wish I knew something worse for a curse."

Faust. " What ails you?"

Mephist. " I would this instant send myself to the devil, if I were not a devil myself!"

Faust. " Is your head turned? How it becomes you to rave like a madman!"

Mephist. " Only think, the ornaments provided for Margaret, are seized by a Friar!—The mother got sight of the articles; she immediately began to be alarmed; for that woman's scent is very keen in distinguishing whether a thing be holy or prophane. " My child," said she, " ill-gotten wealth entraps the soul, and preys upon the vitals. We will devote it to the Mother of God." Margaret made a wry face. The mother sent for a friar, who coveting the jewels, said,

F

you are in the right way: he who conquers is the gainer. The Pope's church has a good stomach, has swallowed whole countries, and yet never was surfeited. The church alone, my good women, can digest ill-gotten wealth."

Faust. " That is a general practice; a Jew and an Emperor can do as much."

Mephist. " Thereupon he pocketed the clasps, chains and rings, like so many mushrooms; returned no more thanks than for a basket of nuts; promised every heavenly reward, and left them much edified."

Faust. " And Margaret?"

Mephist. " Is now sitting full of uneasiness, knowing neither what she wants, nor what she should want, and thinking night and day of the trinkets, but more of him who brought them for her."

Faust. " Get her some other jewels immediately! The first were not of much consequence. And get acquainted with her neighbour."

Mephist. " Yes, my Lord, with all my heart."   [*Exit* Faust.

Mephist. " A fool, when in love, would destroy the sun, the moon, and all the stars in heaven, by way of pastime for his mistress."

[*Exit.*

The Neighbour's House.

Martha (alone). " God forgive my dear husband; he did not use me well, to go into the wide world, and leave me alone. I am sure I never vexed him; I loved him from my heart. (*She weeps.*) Perhaps he is dead! Oh dear! if I had but a certificate of his death!"

Margaret enters, and shews her a casket much more valuable than the first.

Martha. " You must not tell your mother of it; she would take it again to her confessor."

Margaret. " Only see! Only look here!"

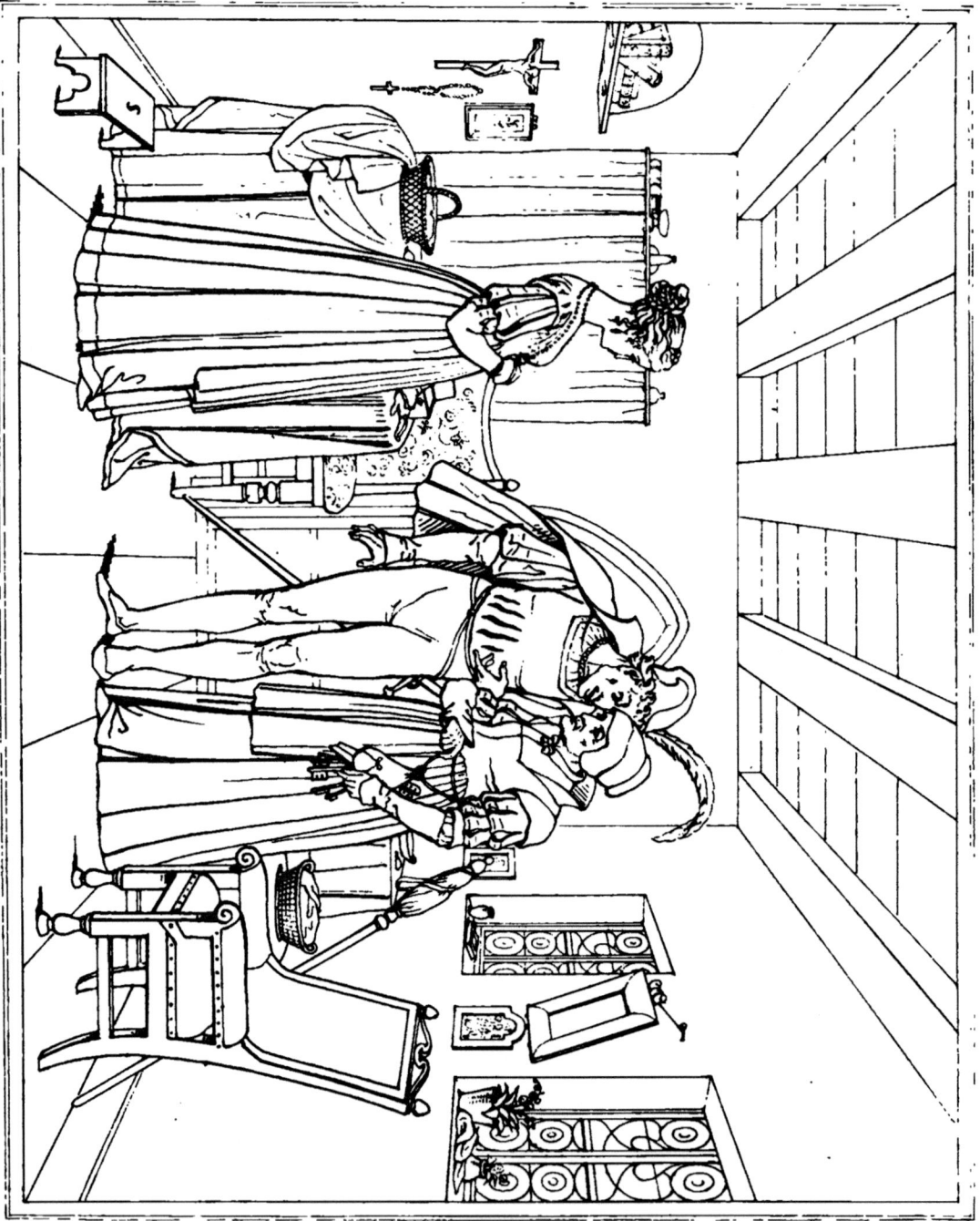

MEPHISTOPHELES INFORMS MARTHA OF HER HUSBANDS DEATH.

Engraved by Henry Moses.

Pl. 13

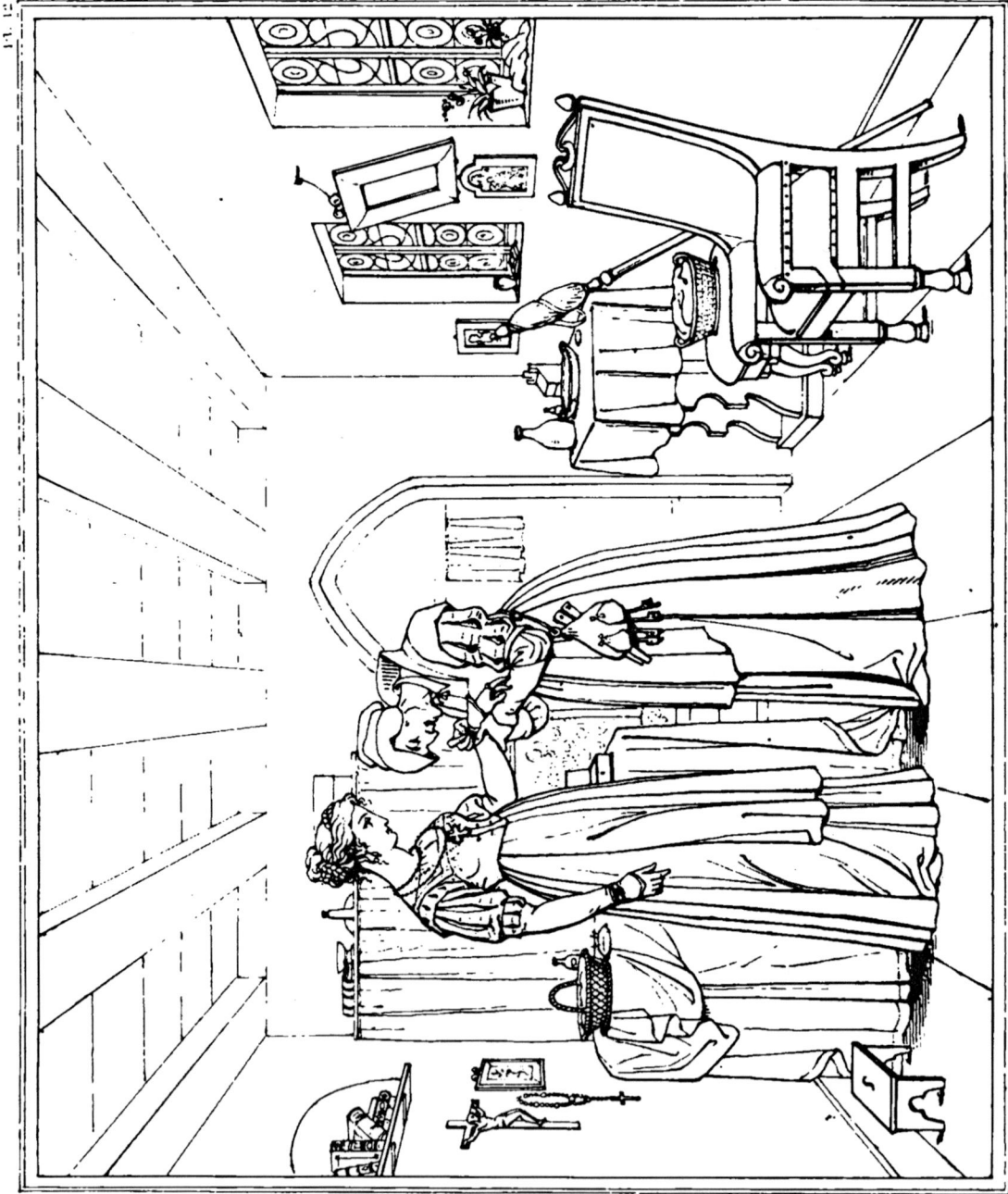

MARGARET SHEWS HER TREASURES TO MARTHA.

Engraved by Henry Moses

Published by Bailey & Sons 4 Broad Street, June 1, 1831.

Martha (putting them on). See Plate XII.—" Oh, thou lucky creature !"

Margaret. " Alas! I dare neither shew myself with them in the street, nor at church."

Martha. " Come to me frequently, and put them on privately; walk up and down for an hour before the looking-glass; we will enjoy it; and then some opportunity will present itself; some festival will happen, at which we may shew them to the people by degrees. Perhaps your mother may not notice it, or we may tell her a story." (*A knock.*)

Margaret. " Oh dear! Perhaps it is my mother."

Martha peeps through the curtain.—" It is a strange gentleman. Walk in!"

Mephist. enters, begs pardon, and asks for Mrs. Martha Swertlein. See Plate XIII.

Martha. " I am she. What is your pleasure, Sir?"

Mephist. (*aside to Martha.*) " I know you now, that is enough for me; you have a noble visitor there; excuse my freedom; I will return in the afternoon."

Martha. " Only think, child, the gentleman takes you for a noble lady."

Margaret. " I am a poor young girl; you are too polite, Sir; the jewels are not mine."

Mephist. tells Martha that her husband is dead, and that he desired to be remembered to her."

Martha weeps, and is almost dying.

Margaret. " Therefore I never wish to love; I should die with grief for such a loss."

Mephist. tells Martha that her husband lies buried at Padua with St. Anthony, in consecrated ground; and to her question, whether he sends her any thing, answers—" Yes, a request of great importance: to cause three hundred masses to be. said for. him. ...For the rest, my pockets are empty."

Martha. " What! not a keepsake? No jewels?"

Mephist. proceeds in his story, that her husband did not waste his money, and that he repented of his faults; the bed on which he died was rather better than a dunghill, being straw half-rotten; his last wish was, that his wife might forgive him for having forsaken her.

Martha (sobbing). " Oh, the good man! I have forgiven him long since."

Mephist. " But, said he, she was more in fault than I."

Martha. " What a liar! To lie so on the verge of. the grave, shocking!"

Mephist. continues telling her, that her husband, when he sailed from Malta, prayed for his wife and children; that his vessel then took a Turkish vessel with treasure for the Grand Signior, and he got a good share of the prize-money.

Martha. " What! Pray where is it? Did he bury it?"

Mephist. " It is all gone. A fair lady took care of him at Naples, and shewed him much kindness, of which he felt the effects to his blessed end."

Martha. " Oh, the villain! the thief to his children! And all his poverty, all his indigence, could not alter his shameful course of life."

Mephist. " You see, he has paid for it with his life. In your place, I would mourn for him a year, and then look out for another husband."

Martha. " Ah! I shall not easily find another like him. He was a good-natured fool: only he liked to rove, and was too fond of foreign women, foreign wine, and the cursed dice."

Mephist. " Well, well! there is no harm, if he connived at you for about as much. I swear, on this condition, I would change rings with you."

Martha. " O, Sir, you are joking!"

Mephist. (*aside.*) " Now it is time to be off. She would tie the devil himself to his word. Farewell, ladies!"

Martha wishes to have some proof of her husband's death."

Mephist. promises to bring a friend to certify it; and assures Margaret, that his friend is very polite to ladies, and has travelled much."

Margaret. " I should blush before the gentleman."

Mephist. " Before no king on earth."

Martha. " We'll expect the two gentlemen this evening in my garden behind the house."

A Street.

FAUST. MEPHISTOPHELES.

Mephist. informs Faust that he shall see Margaret this evening at Martha's, who is just the thing for a bawd and a gypsey; but that they must certify her husband's burial at Padua.

Faust. " Very wisely! We must make the journey first."

Mephist. " Sancta Simplicitas! There is no need of that; only give your evidence without knowing any thing about it."

Faust refuses to do so.

Mephist. " O, holy man! Would it be the first time that you bore false witness? Did you not boldly give definitions of God, the world, motion, man, and the soul? And, if you rightly consider, did you know more about these things than about Mr. Swertlein's death?"

Faust. " You are, and always will be a liar and a sophist."

Mephist. " Yes, if I did not know better. For to-morrow you will not delude poor Margaret. You will then in vain swear the love of your soul to her."

Faust. " But really from my very heart."

A Garden.

MARGARET *on* FAUST's *Arm.*—MARTHA *with* MEPHISTOPHELES,

Walking up and down.

After some indifferent conversation between the two couples as they pass by,—

Faust. " Simplicity, Innocence never knows herself and her sacred value. Humility, meekness, the greatest gifts of kind, bountiful Nature."

Margaret. " Think of me only for a moment; I shall have time enough to think of you."

Faust. " Are you frequently alone?"

Margaret. " Yes, our family is but small, yet it must be attended to. We keep no servant; I am obliged to cook, sweep, knit, and sew, and run about both early and late. And my mother is so particular. Not that she need be so very sparing; for my father has left some property, a small house, and a little garden out of town. My brother is a soldier; my little sister is dead. I had much trouble with that child, but would gladly go through it again, so much I loved her."

Faust. " An angel, if she resembled you."

The conversation goes on between them, and when they pass on, *Mephistopheles* and *Martha* walk by, conversing, and pass on.

Faust. " You knew me again, you little angel, the moment I entered the garden!"

Margaret. " Did you not see? I cast down my eyes."

Faust. " And you forgive the liberty I took—my insolent boldness when you came from church the other day?"

THE DECISION OF THE FLOWER.

Pl. 14.

Margaret. " I was surprized, I had never been served so; no person could speak ill of me. Oh! thought I, did he see in my behaviour any thing forward or improper? He seemed all at once to take it into his head to make up to me. Shall I own it? I could not tell what stirred here immediately in your favour; but, indeed, I was very angry with myself, for not finding it in my heart to be more angry with you."

Faust. " My sweet love!"

Margaret. " Stop a moment."

She plucks a corn-flower, and pulls off the leaves one after the other.

Faust. " What does this mean? A nosegay?"

Margaret. " No, it only means play."

Faust. " How so?"

Margaret. " Done! You'll laugh at me."

She pulls off the leaves, and mutters half aloud.---(See Plate XIV.)--- " He loves me—loves me not—loves me—not—loves me—not."

Tearing of the last leaf with great delight.—" He loves me!"

Faust. Yes, love! Let this decision of the flower be to thee a sentence of the gods. He loves thee! Do you comprehend what that means? He loves thee!"—(He grasps both her hands.)

Margaret. " I tremble!"

Faust. " Oh, tremble not! Let this look, this pressure of your hands, tell you what is beyond expression: To yield ourselves up completely and to feel delight, which must be everlasting! For ever! Its end would be despair! No, without end! without end!"

Margaret presses his hands, disengages herself, and runs away. He stands a moment in thought, then follows her.

Martha coming in. " Night approaches.

Mephist. " Yes, and we will go.

Martha. " I would beg you to stay longer, but this is a very censorious town. The neighbours are as if they had nothing else to do, than to watch one's steps and actions; and we should be slandered, were we ever so careful. And our young couple?"

Mephist. " Have flown up that walk, like sportive butterflies."

Martha. " He seems to be fond of her."

Mephist. " And she of him. That is the way of the world.

<hr>

A summer-house.

Margaret runs in, conceals herself behind the door, places her fingers' ends to her lips, and peeps through the chink. " He is coming!"

Faust enters. " Ah you little rogue, thus you trick me! Did I catch you!" *(He kisses her.)*

Margaret. (*embracing him and returning the kiss.*) (See Plate XV.) " Dearest man! I love thee from my heart!"

Mephistopheles knocks.

Faust. *(stamping with his foot.)* " Who's there?"

Mephist. " A friend!"

Faust. " A beast."

Mephist. " I think it is time to go."

Martha arrives. " Yes, Sir, it is late."

Faust. " May I see you home?"

Margaret. " My mother would---Farewell!"

Faust. " And must I go? Farewell!

Martha. " Adieu!"

Margaret. " Soon to meet again."

[*Exeunt* Faust *and* Mephistopheles.

Margaret. " Dear me! How many things such a man can think! I stand before him ashamed, and say yes to every thing. What a poor ignorant thing I am. I cannot conceive what he can find in me." [*Exit.*

Pl. 15

Engraved by Henry Moses

MARGARET MEETS FAUST IN THE SUMMER HOUSE.

Published by Septimus Prowett Strand Street June 1827.

A Forest and a Cavern.

FAUST *solus.*

" Supreme spirit, thou gavest me all for which I prayed thee. Thou hast not in vain turned thy face towards me in the fire. Thou gavest me glorious nature for a kingdom, and the faculty to feel, to enjoy her. Not merely a chilly gazing visit dost thou permit me; thou grantest me to penetrate into the breast of nature, as into the bosom of a friend. Thou leadest the series of living creatures before me, and teachest me to know my brethren in the silent bush, in the air and water. When the storm howls and cracks in the forest, tears down the gigantic pine, crushing the neighbouring branches and trunks, and when the hill resounds with hollow thunder from its fall, then dost thou lead me to the secure cavern, shewest me myself, and barest the deep and secret wounds of my own breast. And before my view the pale clear moon ascends to the zenith; while from the walls of the rock, arise the silver forms of former ages, issuing from the damp bush, which waving before me, moderates the stern delight of contemplation."

" Oh! Now I feel that perfection is not allotted to man. To this delight,

> Which draws me near and nearer to the gods,
> Thou gavest me, in addition, that companion
> Whom I can no longer do without;
> Though, cold and insolent, he doth debase
> Me to myself, and into naught doth turn,
> With the mere breath of words, thy fairest gift.
> He fans within my breast a madd'ning fire,
> Officious, prompts me to that fairest form.
> Thus from desire I to enjoyment reel,
> And in enjoyment for desire I pant."

G

Enter MEPHISTOPHELES.

Mephist. " Have you now led this kind of life long enough? How can you find pleasure in it long? It will do to taste it once; but then to something fresh!"

Faust. " I wish you had something else to do than to plague me on *a good day.*"

Mephist. " Well! I'll let you alone, you need hardly desire me in earnest. Surely a fellow so unkind, tart and mad, as you are, is no great loss. All day long I have full employment! I can never trace in your looks, Sir, what you like, and what I am not to do."

Faust. " That is just the right tune! You require thanks for being tiresome to me."

Mephist. " Poor son of the earth, how could you lead your life without me?"

Faust. " If you could conceive what new energy of life this living in the wilderness gives me, you would be devil enough to envy me my happiness."

After some further conversation in the same strain, Mephistopheles tells Faust, that his beloved girl sits fretting and moping, and cannot forget him for a moment. At one time she weeps, at another appears composed, but is always in love.

Faust. " Thou serpent !"

Mephist. (aside.) " I lay, I'll catch you!"—

Faust. " Cursed villain! Get thee gone, and name not that fair girl. Do not make my half-maddened senses desire her again!"

Mephist. " She thinks you have forsaken her, and so you have almost."

Faust. " I am near her, were I ever so far off, I can never forget, never lose her."

Pl. 16

MARGARET DISCONSOLATE AT HER SPINNING WHEEL.

Published by Brown & Son, Bristol, 1825

Mephist. " I must laugh. What a pity! You shall go into your fair one's chamber, not to death."

Faust. " What heavenly joy is in her arms! Though I should recline upon her bosom, yet I should always feel her woe. Am I not the fugitive, the houseless wanderer, the barbarian without an object, and without repose, who, like a water-fall, rushes from rock to rock with eager fury. And she, with childlike quiescent passions in the cottage, and all her homely occupations embraced in that little world. And I, hated of God, was not satisfied to seize the rocks and beat them into fragments. Herself, her peace of mind I have undermined! Thou, O hell, didst demand this sacrifice! Help me, devil, to curtail the time of anguish! May the wreck of her fate fall upon me, and may she sink with me."

Mephist. " How you boil and glow again! Go in, you fool, and console her! Where your headstrong little brain discerns no alternative, it fancies directly that the end is come. Long live the brave! In other respects you are pretty well demonized. I know nothing more silly in the world, than a devil who despairs."

Margaret's Chamber.

MARGARET *at the spinning-wheel, alone.* (See Plate XVI.)

Margaret. " My peace of mind is gone, my heart is heavy; I never find repose, ah, never!

" Where I have him not, there is my grave, all the world is the bitterness of gall to me. My poor head is turned, my poor senses are bewildered."

Martha's Garden.

Margaret, Faust.

Margaret. " Promise me, Henry !"

Faust. " Whatever I am able."

Margaret. " Now tell me, how do you stand with religion ? You are a very good man ! but I think, you make very light of religion."

Faust. " Let that alone, my dear child ! you feel that I wish you well ; I would lay down my life for my beloved friends. I will rob no person of his faith and church."

Margaret. " That is not right, you must believe in it !"

Faust. " Must I ?"

Margaret. " Ah ! If I could prevail on you ! And you do not venerate the holy sacraments."

Faust. " I do revere them."

Margaret. " But without desire. You have not been to mass, to confession, this long while. Do you believe in God ?"

Faust. " My dear love, who can say, I believe in God ? Ask the priest, or the philosopher, and their answer is only a scoff at the inquirer."

Margaret. " So you do not believe ?"

Faust. " Do not misinterpret me, sweet face ! Who can name him ? And who can confess, " I believe in him." Who can feel him, and venture to say, " I do not believe in him ?" The Being which embraces all, preserves all. Does he not embrace and preserve thee,—myself,—nay, his own self ? Behold the arched vault of heaven above, the firm earth below, the long enduring stars ascending with friendly ray. I see you eye to eye, and within you every sensation crouds to the head and the heart, and he moves near you invisibly, perceptible in eternal mystery. Replenish your heart therewith, great as it is, and when you feel happy in this sensation, call it bliss, heart, love, God. I have no name for it. Perception is all; nature is but an empty sound, a smoke which obscures the ardent glow of heaven."

Margaret. " All this is very fair and good. The parson says nearly the same thing, only in different words."

Faust. " Every where, all hearts say the same thing, each in its own dialect; why should not I, in mine?"

Margaret. " To hear you, it would appear passable, still it is not right; for you have no Christianity. I have felt very sorry this long time, to see you in such company. The man, whom you have for a companion, is hateful to me, from my inmost soul. Never did any thing give so deadly a stab to my heart as that man's offensive features."

Faust. " Dear child, fear him not."

Margaret. " His presence agitates my blood. I am well-disposed towards all other men ; but much as I long to see you, I have a latent horror of that man ; and, moreover, I take him for a villain ! God forgive me, if I wrong him !"

Faust. " There must be such fellows."

Margaret. " I would not live with any like him. Whenever he comes in, he looks so sneering, and rancorous ; it is plain he feels no interest in any thing; it is written on his forehead, that he can love no person. I feel so happy in your arms, so free, so resignedly warm, but his presence stifles my heart."

Faust. " You foreboding angel !"

Margaret. " It overpowers me so, that when he comes near us, I even fancy I love you no longer ; and when he is here, I could never say my prayers, and that corrodes my heart. You, Henry, must feel the same."

Faust. " You have an antipathy."

Margaret. " Now I must go."

Faust. " Ah! can I never cling to your bosom for a single hour, press you to my bosom and thus unite our souls?

Margaret. " If I did but sleep alone! I would leave the bolt open for you this night, but my mother does not sleep soundly, and if she should catch us, she would kill me directly."

Faust. " My angel, there is no fear of that. Here is a vial! only three drops poured in her drink, will kindly envelop nature in deep slumber."

Margaret. " What would I not do for your sake? I hope it will do her no harm?"

Faust. " Would I recommend it to you, if it would, my love?"

Margaret. " When I do but look at you, dear love, I do not know what prompts me to your will; I have done so much for you already, that there is hardly any thing left." [*Exit.*

Enter MEPHISTOPHELES.

Mephist. " The grass-ape! Is she gone?"

Faust. " Have you been listening again?"

Mephist. " I have fully heard how the doctor was catechized; much good may it do you."

Faust. " Thou monstrous villain! dost not see, how this faithful, loving soul, full of her faith, (the only saving one as she fancies,) holily torments herself with the thought that the man she most loves should perish."

Mephist. " And she understands physiognomy like a master. In my presence she feels uncomfortable, my mask hides a lurking fiend, perhaps, even the devil. Well, to-night?---"

Faust. " What is that to you?"

Mephist. " I shall laugh in my sleeve."

MARGARET MEDITATING THE MATER DOLOROSA.

PL 17

At a Pump.

MARGARET *and* BETSEY *with pitchers.*

Betsey tells Margaret that Barbara, being pregnant, is to do penance at church.

Margaret pities her, and walking home by herself, reflects upon her own strict censoriousness formerly, whilst she now is fallen in sin herself.

THE FAUSSEBRAYE.

In the niche of the wall is an image of the Mater dolorosa; before it are some flower-pots. (See Plate XVII.)

Margaret, (puts fresh flowers in the pot.) " O thou full of sorrow, graciously incline thy face to my woe!

" A sword pierces thy heart, thou lookest up with a thousand pangs, to see thy dying son.

" My heart will break.

" I bedewed with my tears, the potsherds in my window, when, early in the morn, I culled thee these flowers."

NIGHT.

The street near Margaret's door.

Valentine, a soldier, Margaret's brother. This brave and honest soldier relates what a paragon of virtue and beauty his sister was, and how he always used to praise her before all men. But now every villain jeers, sneers at, and insults him. He must sit at his liquor as mute as a bad debtor, and though he were to knock them down, he cannot call them liars. " Who comes there sneaking? If I see right, there be two of them. If it be he, I'll be at him, he shall not escape alive !"

FAUST, MEPHISTOPHELES.

Mephistopheles plays the guitar, and sings a serenade.

Valentine advances, " Whom dost thou allure here, thou cursed rat-catcher ! I will first send thy instrument to the devil, and then the singer after it !"

He breaks the guitar, and fights with *Faust.*

Mephistopheles parries the blows.

Valentine. " Parry this !"

Mephist. " Why not?"

Valentine. " And this?"

Mephist. " Certainly !"

Valentine. " I think the devil fights ! How is this? My hand feels lamed."

Mephist. (to Faust.) " Now strike." (See Plate XIX.)

Valentine drops down. " Oh heavens !"

Mephist. " Now the looby is tamed. We must be off, and disappear, for a murderous hue and cry is set up. I can manage the police surprisingly, but never the criminal law."

Martha, at her window. " Come out! Come out!"

Margaret, at her own window. " Bring a light."

People. " There lies a dead man !"

Martha, coming out, " Are the murderers fled?"

Margaret, coming out. " Who is lying there?"

People. " Your mother's son." (See Plate XX.)

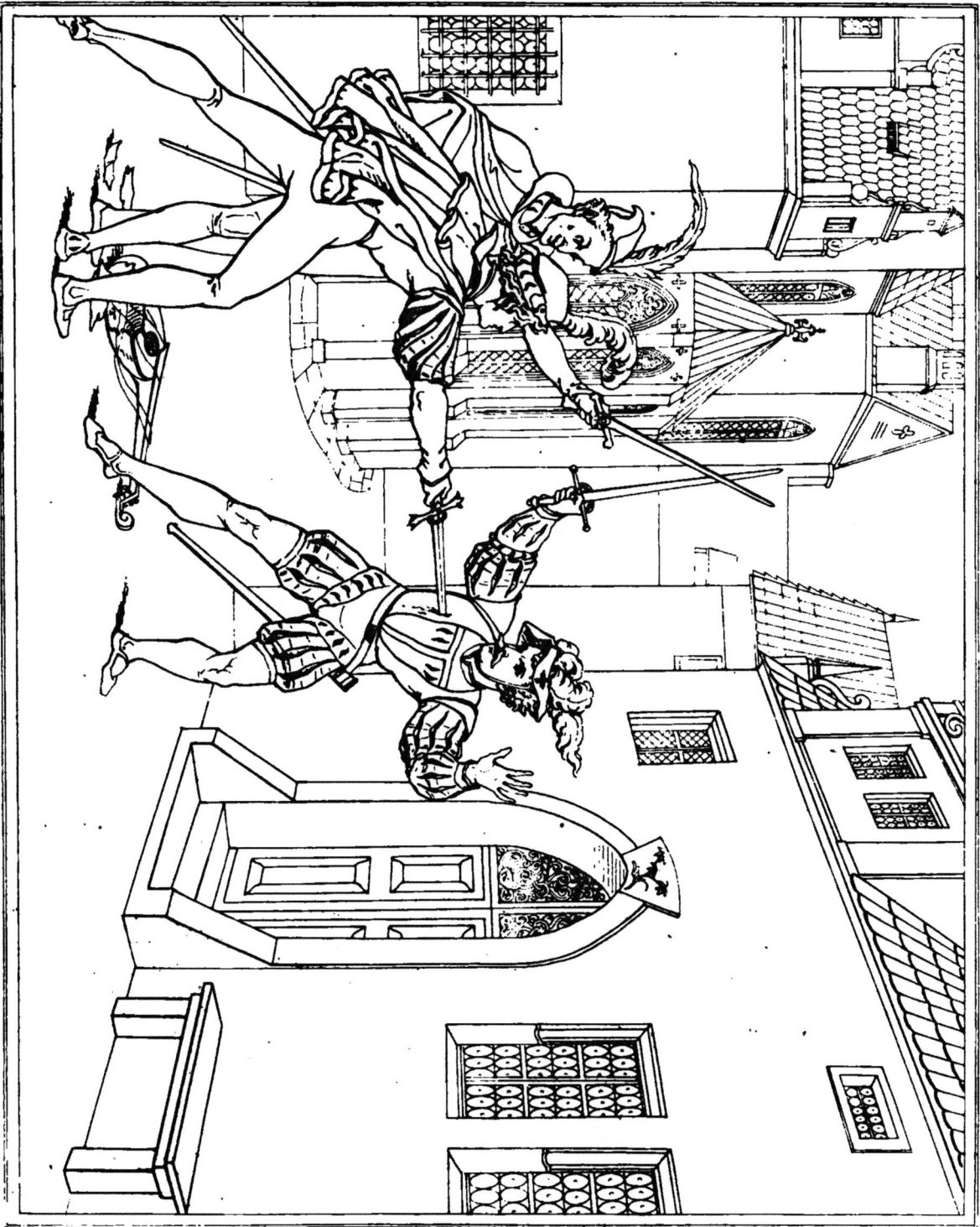

VALENTINE FIGHTS WITH FAUST.

Engraved by Henry Moses.

Published by ... & Sons, Broad Street, July 1830.

Pl. 19

VALENTINE DYING REPROACHES MARGARET.

Engraved by Henry Moser

Published by Henry Colten, 4 Bread Street July 1 1850

Valentine. " I die! That is soon said, and sooner done. Women, why do you stand wailing and lamenting? Come near, and hear me. *(All the people flock round him.)*

" My Margaret, see! you are young, you are yet very foolish, and your conduct is much to blame. I only tell you in confidence, that after all, you are now ruined past recovery."

Margaret. " My brother! Oh God! What do you mean?"

Valentine. " Do not profane the name of God: what is done cannot be recalled, and things will take their course. You commenced with one in private; soon will others be at you; and when you have had a dozen, the whole town has got you.

" When Infamy is born, she is brought into the world privately, and the veil of night is pulled over her head and ears; nay, you would wish to kill her: but when she grows up, she walks about barefaced, even by day, and yet is not grown more comely. The more ugly her face grows, the more she seeks the day-light. And though God may forgive thee, thou wilt be cursed on earth."

Martha. " Recommend your soul to the mercy of God! Would you heap scandal upon you?"

Valentine. " Oh, if I could but reach your withered carcase, you infamous procuress, then should I hope to obtain full forgiveness for all my sins!"

Margaret. " My brother! What torment!"

Valentine. " Leave off crying. You then gave my heart the deepest wound, when you abandoned your honour. I go, through the sleep of death, to God, like a soldier and a brave man."---*(Dies.)*

H

THE CATHEDRAL CHURCH.

Mass, Organ, and Singing.

MARGARET amongst a numerous congregation. The EVIL SPIRIT behind Margaret·

Evil Spirit. " How very differently did you feel, Margaret, when you approached the altar, full of innocence; when you stammered out your prayers from the worn-out book, your heart half occupied with childrens' play, half with God. How stands thy head? In thy heart, what misdeeds! Dost thou pray for thy mother's soul, who, through thee, slumbered on to long, long torment?—whose blood was spilt on thy threshold?

Margaret. " Woe! Woe! Could I but get rid of the thoughts which perplex and accuse me!"

Chorus.

" Dies irae, dies illa
Solvet sæclum in favilla."

A sound of the organ.

Evil Spirit. " Wrath seizes thee! The trumpet sounds! The graves shake! And thy spirit, created afresh from mouldering ashes, ascends with trembling!"

Chorus.

" Judex ergo cum sedebit,
Quidquid latet apparebit,
Nil inultum remanebit."

Margaret. " I feel so oppressed! The wall-pillars inclose me! The vault weighs down upon me! Oh, for breath!"

FAUST AND MEPHISTOPHELES ASCEND THE BROKEN.

Engraved by Henry Moses.

Published by Boosey & Sons 4 Broad Street, July 1 1820.

Page 98 the Second Part.

THE EVIL SPIRIT WHISPERS DESPAIR TO MARGARET WHILE AT MASS

Published by Boosey & Sons, 4 Bread Street, Cheapside.

Evil Spirit. " Hide thyself! Sin and infamy cannot be hid. Breath! Light! Woe to thee!''

Chorus.

" Quid sum miser tunc dicturus?
Quem patronum rogaturus?
Cum vix justus sit securus."

Evil Spirit. " The glorified blessed souls turn their face away from thee : the pure souls shudder to give thee their hand. Woe!'' (See Plate XVIII.)

Chorus.

" Quid sum miser tunc dicturus?''

Margaret. " Neighbour! Your smelling-bottle." *(She faints.)*

WALPURGIS NIGHT.

The Hartz Mountains.

The Region of the Schirke and Elend.

FAUST. MEPHISTOPHELES.

Mephist. " Do you not want a broomstick? I should like to ride on a goat. In this way we make but a slow progress."

Faust prefers walking with his knotty stick, and clambering over the rocks.

Mephist. asks an Ignis Fatuus to skip before them, lighting the way. (See Plate XXI.)

The *Ignus Fatuus* skips before them in a zig-zag direction, just as men do, never straight forward.

Faust, Mephistopheles, Ignis Fatuus, singing a trio.

" It seems we have entered into the spheres of dreams and witches. Conduct us well!''

Mephistopheles shews Faust a treasure glowing in a deep cleft of the mountain.

A chorus of *witches* riding to the Brocken through the air, on goats, on sows, broomsticks, pitchforks, in baking-troughs, &c.

Mephistopheles is quite in his own element, and on this gala (as men shew their stars and badges) will not remain incognito, but exhibits his foot.

Faust compares the revels to a fair. *Mephistopheles* points out to him *Lilith,* Adam's first wife.

Faust dances with a young witch, and talks of the apples in Paradise (meaning the forbidden fruit, which the ignorant imagine to have been an apple; but it is not likely that the same fruit, (for the literal text is true,) should be now found out of Paradise upon earth.)

Mephistopheles dances with an old witch.

A *Proctophantasmist,* or one of the Illuminati, is much vexed that he cannot make the witches and ghosts disappear. He cannot bear the despotism of spirits, and hopes yet to conquer devils and poets.

Mephist. says that the Proctophantasmist will sit down in a quagmire, which is his usual way of solacing himself, and when the leeches feast on him, will be cured of spirits and conceit.

Faust quits his fair dancer, because a red mouse leaped out of her mouth, and then says to Mephistopheles :—(See Plate XXII.)

" Mephisto, do you see yonder that pale, beautiful girl, standing alone, and at a distance? She drags herself slowly on, and seems to walk with fettered legs. I must own that I think she resembles my kind Margaret."

Mephist. tells him it is a mere lifeless, magical apparition, which it is not proper to accost—as it would chill the blood, and that to every man she appears like his own love. That, like Medusa, she will turn men into stone, and can carry her head under her arm, since Perseus has cut it off.

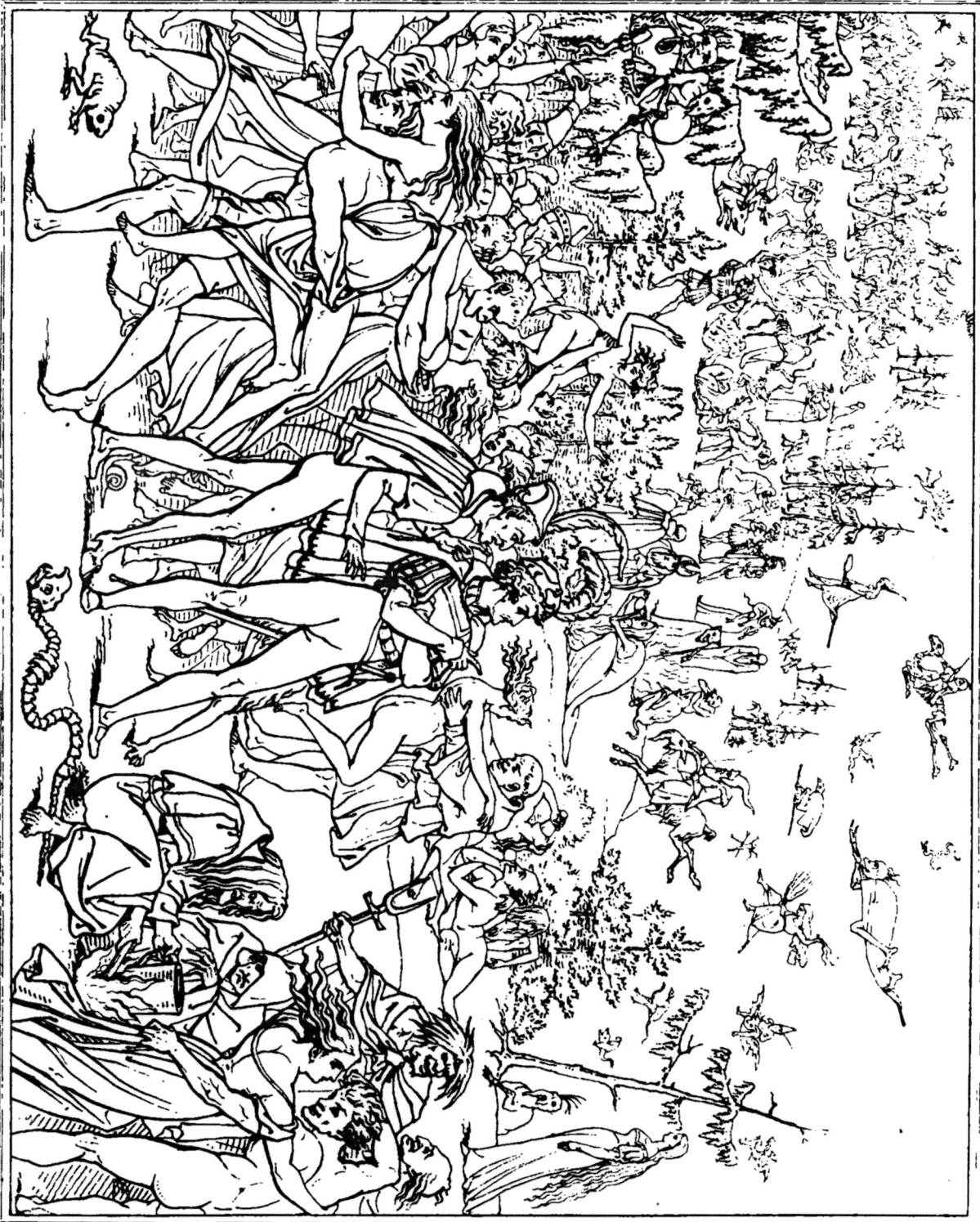

Engraved by Henry Moses.

THE WITCHES REVEL.

Published by Henry Colburn, & Richard Bentley, New Burlington Street, 1830.

Pl. 22

Faust cannot take off his eyes, and with melancholy feelings remembers his own Margaret—he sees a narrow red string round her neck. They proceed to a stage, where a play, by some Dilettanti, is announced.

Mephistopheles greatly approves to find the actors on the Blocksberg, that being the proper place to which they belong.

Dream of the Walpurgis-night, or OBERON's *and* TITANIA's *Golden Wedding.*

AN INTERLUDE.

(This sprightly Interlude, replete with wit and satire, has no connection with the Tragedy, and is therefore omitted here.)

A GLOOMY DAY.

The Country.

FAUST. MEPHISTOPHELES.

Faust. " In wretchedness! despairing! for a long time miserably weltering on the ground, and now in a prison! That gentle unhappy creature, like a malefactor confined in prison, and reserved for dreadful torments! To this pitch! this extremity!—Traitor, vile spirit, and this thou hast concealed from me! Thou mayest stand furiously rolling about thy diabolical eyes! Stand, bidding me defiance with thy unbearable presence!—Imprisoned! In irrecoverable misery! Delivered up to evil spirits, and to vindictive, unfeeling judges! And all the whilst thou lulledst me with the most insipid diversions, concealing from me her increasing misery, and leaving her to perish unrelieved!"

Mephist. " She is not the first." (See Plate XXIII.)

Faust. " Thou dog! Abominable monster! Transform him, oh infinite spirit! Again transform the reptile into his canine form, in which he frequently took pleasure in trotting on before me—in rolling before the feet of the harmless pedestrian, and clinging to his shoulders when falling. Transform him again into his favourite form, that he may crawl on his belly in the dust, and that I may tread him under my feet, the vile reprobate! Not the first! A woeful pity! Too much for any human soul to conceive, that more than one creature should be sunk into this depth of misery; that the first in her writhing agonies should not suffice in the eyes of the forgiving eternal spirit to atone for the guilt of all the rest. The sufferings of this one person harrow up my soul, and thou sneerest coolly at the fate of thousands."

Mephist. " Now we are again at our wit's end, where you, human beings, overstrain your senses. Why do you engage with us in a compact, if you cannot go through with it? You want to fly, and are not proof against giddiness. Did we officiously intrude upon you, or you upon us?"

Faust. " Do not shew me your voracious teeth! I detest you! Supreme glorious spirit, who hast deigned to reveal thyself to me, thou who knowest my heart and my very soul, why tie me with chains to this shameful villain—this miscreant, who seeks his delight in mischief, his enjoyment in destruction?"

Mephist. " Have you done?"

Faust. " Preserve her! or woe be to you! The most horrid curse upon you for many thousand years!"

Mephist. " I cannot loosen the bonds of the avenger, nor open his bolts—Preserve her! Who was it that plunged her into destruction—I, or you?"

Faust looks about him wildly.

FAUST HEARS THAT MARGARET IS IN PRISON.

Engraved by Henry Moses

PL. 25

Engraved by Henry Moore

MEPHISTOPHELES AND FAUST PASS THE PLACE OF EXECUTION.

Mephist. " Are you going to grasp the thunder ? It is well that it was not given to you, miserable mortals !"

Faust. " Take me to her, she shall be free !"

Mephist. " And the danger to which you expose yourself. Know that the guilt of blood from your hand still remains upon the town. Over the grave of the slain hover the avenging spirits, and watch for the murderer's return."

Faust. " This also from thee? The murder and death of a world be upon thee, thou miscreant! Take me to her, I say, and deliver her !"

Mephist. " I'll conduct you, and what I can do, you shall hear. Have I all power in heaven and on earth? The jailor's senses I will intoxicate ; you seize the keys, and lead her out by the hand of a man. I will await you. The magic horses stand ready ; I will carry you off. This is what I am able to perform."

Faust. Quick let us be off then !"

Night.   The open Country.

FAUST---MEPHISTOPHELES---*rushing by on black horses.*
(See Plate XXIV.)

Faust. " What are those creatures doing that hover about yon place of execution?"

Mephist. " I know not what they are boiling and preparing."

Faust. " They hover up and down, and stoop and bow."

Mephist. " A company of witches."

Faust. " They strew and consecrate."

Mephist. " On ! on !"

A Prison.

Faust, with a bunch of keys and a lamp at an iron door.---He seizes the the lock and opens it. (See Plate XXV.)

Faust. " She suspects not that her beloved listens, that he hears the jingling of the chains, the rustling of the straw." *(He enters.)*

Margaret tries to conceal herself on the couch of straw. " Woe! Woe! They are coming. Bitter death!

Faust, softly. " Hush! hush! I come to release you."

Margaret. (throwing herself before him.) " If you are a human creature have pity on my distress!"

Faust. "You will awake the keepers by your screams." *(He lays hold of the chains to unlock them.)*

Margaret, (on her knees.) " Who gave thee, hangman, this authority over me? You come already to fetch me away at midnight: Have mercy on me, and let me live a little longer! Is it not time enough to-morrow morning? *(She stands up.)* I am so young, so young! And must die already! I was beautiful too, and that was my ruin. My friend was near, now he is far off; the garland lies torn, the flowers are scattered. Do not seize me so forcibly! Spare me! What have I done to you? Let me not supplicate in vain, for I never saw you in my life."

Faust. " Can I survive this agony?"

Margaret. " I am now entirely in your power. Only let me first suckle the infant. I kissed it all night; they have taken it away to distract me, and now they say that I killed it. I shall never know joy again. They sing ballads of me! It is wicked of the people! An old tale ends so: who told them to apply it?"

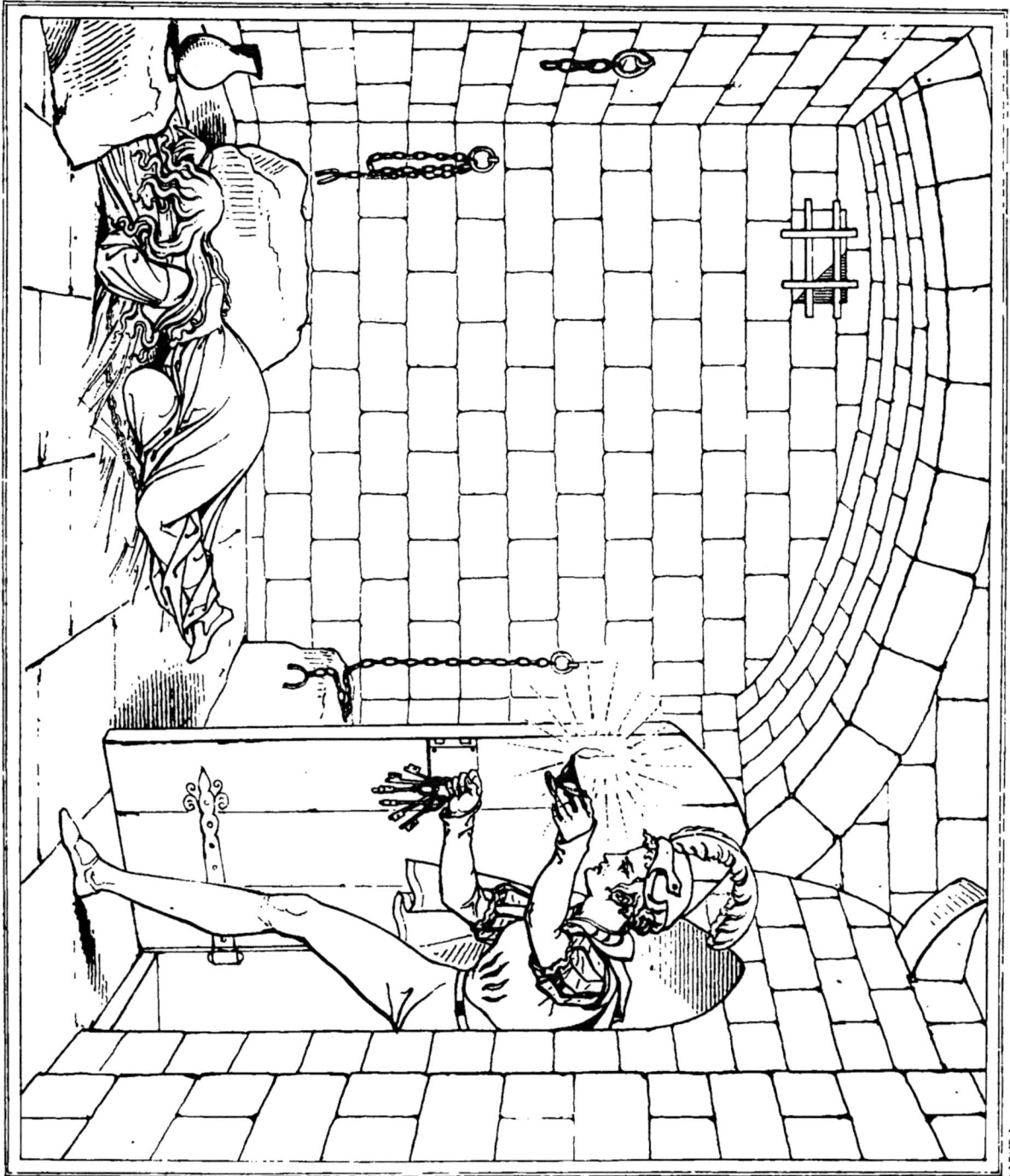

FAUST ENTERS THE PRISON WHERE MARGARET IS.

Engraved by Henry Moses

Published by Reeves & Sons, 6 Bread Street Hill, London.

PL. 24

Faust. (down on his knees.) " A lover lies at your feet to unlock the bondage of woe."

Margaret. (kneels down by him.) " Oh, let us kneel to invoke the saints! Behold! Under these steps, under the threshold, boils hell! The evil spirit roars with horrid wrath."

Faust. (aloud.) " Margaret! Margaret!"

Margaret. (listening) " That was the voice of my friend! *(she jumps up. The chains drop off.)* Where is he? I heard him call. I am free! None shall prevent me. I will fly to his neck, lie on his bosom! He called Margaret! He stood on the threshold. Through the midst of the howlings and din of hell, through the grim, diabolical jeering scoffs, I recognized the sweet, the fond voice."

Faust. " 'Tis I!"

Margaret. " 'Tis you! O say it once more! *(taking hold of him.)* It is he! What is become of pain? What is become of the anguish of the jail? Of the chains? It is then you? Do you come to save me? I am preserved!—There is the street where I saw you for the first time, and the peaceful garden where I and Martha expected you."

Faust. (striving to get her away.) " Come along with me! Come along!"

Margaret. " Oh, tarry! Now I so fondly tarry where you are." *(in an endearing manner.)*

Faust. " Hasten! If you do not make haste, you will suffer for it severely."

Margaret. " What! You cannot kiss any more? My friend, so short a time away from me, and you have forgot kissing? What makes me so fearful on your neck, when formerly your words, your looks, were like heaven to me, and you kissed me as if you would smother me. Kiss me, or else I shall kiss you! *(she embraces him. Alas! Your lips are chilly, they are mute. What is become of your love? Who robbed me of it?" *(she turns away from him.)*

I

Faust. " Come! Follow me! My love, take courage! I'll kiss you with ardour a thousand-fold; but follow me! I pray you do!"

Margaret. (*turning to him.*) " And is it you?   Is it you indeed?"

Faust. " It is I! Come along!"

Margaret. " You loosen the fetters, you take me again on your lap.   How comes it you do not shun me?---And do you know, my friend, whom you liberate?"

Faust. " Come! Come! Night passes away."

Margaret. " I have killed my mother, I have drowned my infant. Was it not given to you and to me? Yes, to you likewise.---It is you! I can hardly believe it.   Give me your hand! It is no dream! Your dear hand!---But it feels moist! Wipe it off! I think there is some blood on it.   Ah God! What have you done! Sheathe your sword, I pray you!"

Faust. " Let the past be forgotten: you kill me."

Margaret. " No, you must remain alive! I will describe the tombs to you.   You must look after them to-morrow without fail; give the best place to my mother, my brothers next to her, mine a little aside, but not too far distant, and the infant must lay on my right breast; else none would lie near me!---To cling to your side used to be a sweet, a delightful happiness! But I am not able now; it seems to me as if I approached you reluctantly, as if you pushed me back; and yet it is you, and you look so good, so virtuous."

Faust. " If you feel it is I, come!"

Margaret. " Whither?"

Faust. " To liberty."

Margaret. " If the grave is without, if death lies in wait; come! From hence to the everlasting bed of rest, and not one step further.--- Are you going now? O Henry, I wish I could go with you!"

Faust. " You can! Only will it! The door stands open."

Margaret. " I dare not go; there is no hope for me.   What avails

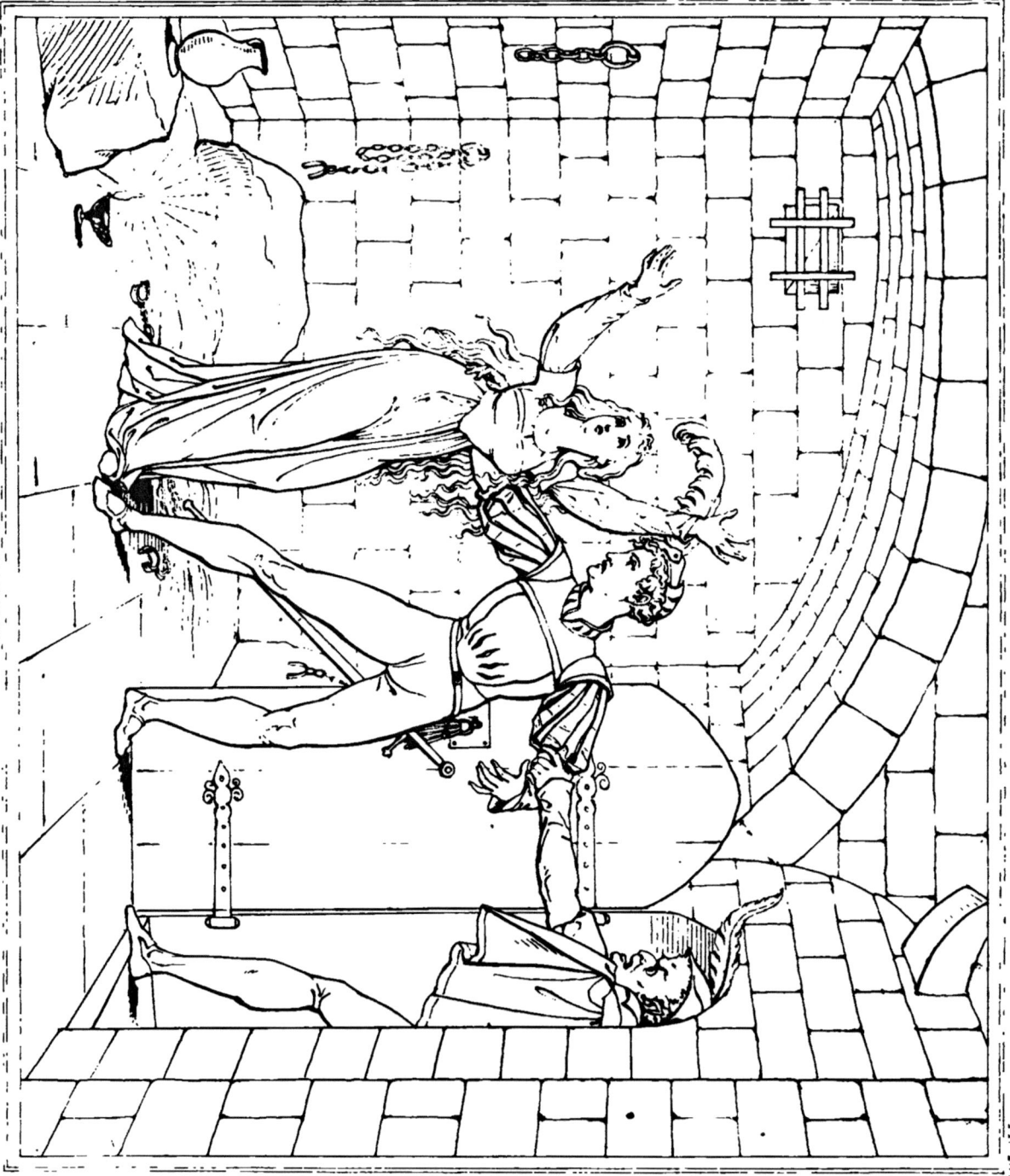

MARGARET REFUSES TO LEAVE THE PRISON.

flight? They lie in wait for me. It is so miserable to be obliged to go begging alms, and above all with a guilty conscience. It is so miserable to wander about in a foreign land; and they will seize me after all."

Faust. I will stay with you.

Margaret. " Quick! Quick! Preserve your poor infant. On! That way up the brook, into the forest, over the stile, to the left where that plank is in the pond. Catch it immediately! It wants to rise, it struggles still! Save it! Save it!"

Faust. " Recollect yourself! Only one step and you are free."

Margaret. " If we were but past that mountain! There sits my mother on a stone and shakes her head; she beckons not, she does not nod, her head feels heavy; she slept so long; she wakes no more: she slept that we should enjoy pleasure. Those were happy times!"

Faust. " The day dawns! My love! My dear!"

Margaret. " The day! Yes, the day dawns; the last day comes: it was to have been my wedding-day! Tell nobody you were with Margaret. We shall meet again, but not at the dance. The crowd presses; she is not heard. The square, the streets cannot hold them. The bell tolls, the judge's wand is broken. How they seize and tie me! I am taken to the block. Now the sword is wielded to behead me. The world lies mute as the grave!"

Faust. " Oh, I wish I had never been born!"

Mephist. is seen without. " Come! or you are lost. (See Plate XXVI.) Useless trembling, delaying; and my horses are shivering: the morning dawns."

Margaret. " What is that ascending from the earth?---He! he! Send him away! What does he want in this holy place? He comes for me!"

Faust. " You shall live.

Margaret. " Judgment of God ! To thy tribunal I surrender my-self !"

Mephist. to Faust. " Come ! Come ! I shall leave you in the lurch with her."

Margaret. " Oh father, I am thine ! Save me ! Ye angels! Ye sainted hosts, pitch your camp around me, to protect me! Henry ! I fear you."

Mephist. " She has been judged !"

A voice from above. " She is preserved !"

Mephist to Faust. " Come to me !" (*disappears with Faust.*)

A voice from within, gradually abating. " Henry ! Henry !"

ERRATA.

Page 13, line 1, *for* " threat," *read* " thereat."
— ib. — 7, *for* " Hippotamus," *read* " Hippopotamus."
— ib. — 9, *for* " spirit," *read* " spirits."
— 15, — 20, *for* " flees," *read* " fleas."
— 26, — *for* " cavern," *read* " kitchen."
— 39, — 17, *for* " of," *read* " off."
Plate VI. *for* " cave," *read* " kitchen."

THE END.

W. WILSON, PRINTER, GREVILLE-STREET, HATTON-GARDEN, LONDON.

LIST OF PLATES.

LaVergne, TN USA
02 August 2010
191768LV00008B/4/P